C000039140

Thriving in the Grace of God

Phil Whitehead

Sovereign World

Sovereign World Ltd
PO Box 777
Tonbridge
Kent TN11 0ZS
England

All Scripture quotations are taken from the New King James Bible
unless otherwise stated. © 1982 by Thomas Nelson Publishers Inc.
Nashville, USA.

Quotations marked NIV are taken from the New International Version
Copyright © 1973, 1978, 1984 International Bible Society.

ISBN 1-85240-406-X

The publishers aim to produce books which will help to extend and
build up the Kingdom of God. We do not necessarily agree with every
view expressed by the author, or with every interpretation of Scripture
expressed. We expect each reader to make his/her judgement in the
light of their own understanding of God's Word and in an attitude of
Christian love and fellowship.

Cover design by CCD, www.ccdgroup.co.uk
Typeset by CRB Associates, Reepham, Norfolk
Printed in the United States of America

"For by grace you have been saved through faith,
and that not of yourselves;
it is the gift of God, not of works,
lest anyone should boast."
(Ephesians 2:8–9)

". . . the gospel of the grace of God."
(Acts 20:24 NIV)

Dedication

I would like to dedicate this book to my ever-loving wife
Caroline without whose support and help, as well as passion
for the message of grace, this book would not have been
possible.

Contents

Acknowledgements

I couldn't begin a book on grace without expressing my immense gratitude to my Heavenly Father whose unfailing grace never fails to astound me.

There are so many who I would like to thank who have given so much to bring this book to publication. Firstly my mother Ruth Warner, through her prayers and Christian upbringing I found Christ. Lyndon Bowring, whose gracious example and attentive advice has been so valuable, and for writing such an excellent foreword. Wynne Lewis, whose enthusiasm for the book and corrections to my many grammatical errors was invaluable. To Brian Richardson, Becky Mitchell, William Atkinson and Vicky Taylor for reading the early drafts and for encouraging me to press on to publication. Adrianne Kalfopoulou for allowing us to stay in her beautiful island house. Tim Pettingale and all at Sovereign World, for their enthusiastic backing of this book.

To Rod Anderson, Trevor Baker, Dr R.T. Kendall and Martin Scott whose support and endorsement of the book has meant so much to me.

To our church family Chiswick Christian Centre, who released me to write the book and who have always been so prayerfully supportive.

Foreword

C.S. Lewis summed up the uniqueness of Christianity in just one word: 'grace'. Our precious inheritance, from the New Testament onwards, is rooted in the doctrine that we are saved by grace alone. Here is the very heart of the Gospel; that we can never work our way into God's favour through deeds but must simply place our trust in what he has done for us through His death and resurrection.

I have known Phil Whitehead for many years. He is a gracious man with a heart for God and a passion for mission, eminently eligible to write on this subject. Reading this book gives us a deeper appreciation of the truth about grace – how it pours from the heart of God into us, spilling over in our lives to bless others.

Grace is about receiving blessings we don't deserve and could never earn, and experiencing it daily in so many areas of our lives – through material provision, physical protection, emotional peace and spiritual power. Forgiveness, cleansing and grace begin at the cross of Christ, where He became sin that we might receive the righteousness of God.

The great commentary on the person of Jesus Christ, found in John's Gospel, is that He was *'full of grace and truth'*. We can sometimes be such sticklers for truth that we focus on sound doctrine and often fail to show His grace. When the Church speaks and acts with grace and ministers to people's deepest needs there will be a hunger for the truth that lies behind the giving, forgiving and thanksgiving they experience. We witness the life-giving heartbeat of God's grace throughout the life and teaching of Jesus, on through the epistles to the last pages of the Book of Revelation.

The story of Jesus' rescue of a woman caught in the act of adultery is a wonderful exposition of grace. The scribes and Pharisees wanted to test His allegiance to the Law of Moses – that adulterers should be stoned to death – and so they dragged this unfortunate woman into the Temple where Jesus was teaching the people, demanding His judgement of her. Her case provided a perfect opportunity to catch Jesus out. Jesus' response was to invite any of the accusers who were without sin to begin the stoning. They all went away and left Him and the trembling defendant alone. Her life was saved and only at that point did Jesus speak of the moral issue; forgiving her and telling her to sin no more. Grace first, then the truth.

You will not find anything approaching the Christian concept of 'grace' in any other religion or philosophy in the world, most of which focus on searching for and attaining perfection through knowledge and good works. But as Phillip Yancey has said, speaking of grace: 'There's nothing you can do to make God love you more and there's nothing you can do to make Him love you less.' The more we are inspired by the glorious truth of His amazing grace the more it will be reflected in our conduct. 1 Corinthians 13 is the way of grace: being patient and kind; not jealous, boastful, arrogant nor rude, neither insisting on our own way, nor irritable, resentful, always rejoicing in what is right, bearing all things, ever hopeful and staying the course to the very end.

If you read and inwardly digest this book you will thrive anew in the grace of God. I've read it twice and it impacted me more the second time!

Rev. Lyndon Bowring

Introduction

When we look at what makes Christianity distinct from
other faiths, a number of things come immediately to mind:
God's bodily incarnation in Christ, the resurrection, the
indwelling of the Holy Spirit within the believer to name
just a few. However, when the great Christian apologist
C.S. Lewis was asked the question, he simply replied,
"grace." Many Christians are familiar that it is "by grace"
we are saved, but have little concept of its ongoing
importance to our lives. For some the teaching on grace is a
soft message we should soon graduate from. This is a sad
misconception, as no matter how holy and sanctified we
become, we will never graduate out of grace. Whoever
we become, our daily relationship with Christ is utterly
dependent on His grace.

Coming from an evangelical background, when I finally
came to faith in Christ I had little difficulty believing my
sins were forgiven. However, I soon encountered a deep
ongoing struggle with how I thought the Father saw me. I
perceived Him as largely against me, looking to
continuously judge my many faults and failings. One effect
of this was that I threw myself into Christian service in the
hope that somehow I might finally gain His acceptance and

approval. Sadly, I became all the more aware of my failings and how far short I constantly fell, even from my own standards. Soon I began to resign myself to a Christian life on earth that, whilst assuring me of my ultimate salvation, was to be lived under a cloud of perpetual condemnation. Though I had received the good news of the gospel, I could never see my life actually becoming much in the way of good news. Unhappily I was not much of an advert for the gospel.

Gradually however I began to discover that my heavenly Father saw me not as I saw myself, but rather in my redemptive position "in Christ"; not attained by my work or performance, but rather a gift given to me by faith right at the start of my Christian life. Little by little I began to see myself differently. Gradually an overriding weight of condemnation began to lift off my life. The incredible verse *"For He made Him who knew no sin to be sin for us, that we might become the righteousness of God in Him"* (2 Corinthians 5:21) steadily became a real personal revelation to me. Slowly but surely I became secure in my walk before the Father.

As I realised that my position as a believer was a beautiful gift received by faith, I began to be more and more aware that the whole foundation of my life was His grace – His unmerited favour upon me. Slowly over time, a fuller awareness of His grace began to permeate through to seemingly every part of my Christian life and began to affect me in numerous different ways. If I had been so undeservedly given this standing by my Father, then my work for Him was no longer an attempt to earn a right standing with God, but rather a thankful outworking of my

full and total acceptance. Now I saw how gracious the
Father had been to me, I began to become more gracious to
others, seeing them in a whole new light. Over time grace
literally transformed my understanding of the Christian life.
Grace was no longer just the starting point quickly to be
moved on from, but the foundation of not only all that I
am, but all that I do. Grace became to me totally pervasive.

Today so many seem to be struggling to really accept His
grace towards them, seeing God only in a condemnatory
and judgemental way. Others, having struggled to embrace
God's grace have opted for a law-bound regulatory
existence that has relegated them to a life far below the
abundant life Christ came to give them. Sadly, when we as
Christians fail to really receive the fullness of Christ's grace,
we do the world a grave disservice and can actually become
a barrier to the gospel. My hope is that we will discover
grace in a much broader sense and that this will be reflected
through us into a world without any real concept of it.

Grace is so all encompassing that no single word or
sentence could successfully describe it. Coming from the
Greek word *charis* it has been described as, "kindness,
mercy, goodwill; the underserved favour and blessings of
God; the depth and richness of the heart and mind of God;
the kindness and love that dwells within the very nature of
God. God's grace covers all of life." Other attempts to
express it include:

> "Grace means all the favours and gifts of God. It means
> all the good and perfect gifts of God, all the good and
> beneficial things He gives us and does for us, whether
> physical, material, or spiritual (James 1:17)."[1]

> "No other word so expresses the depth and richness of the heart and mind of God. This is the distinctive difference between God's grace and man's grace. Whereas man sometimes does favours for his friends and thereby can be said to be gracious, God has done a thing unheard of among men: He has given His very own Son to die for His enemies (Romans 2:11–15)."[2]

> "The word 'undeserved' is the key to understanding grace. Man does not deserve God's favour; he cannot earn God's approval and blessings."[3]

Clearly grace is enormously broad in both definition and application in our lives, so more than a casual glance is required to completely comprehend it.

I remember being given a guided tour around the National Gallery. My normal practice with paintings is to give them a momentary glace of appreciation. However, as the guide talked through the background and detail of each painting, they became much more alive to me. I began to understand and appreciate what the artist was trying to express. It's my heartfelt prayer that as we explore God's grace from a variety of angles, that grace will become more and more alive in you.

Notes

1. Wordsearch, *Discipleship Library Program*, "Practical Word Sudies in the New Testament", Commentary on Ephesians 1:2 (www.wordsearchbible.com).
2. Ibid.
3. Ibid., Commentary on 1 Peter 1:2.

Chapter 1

From Exile to the King's Palace

The End Has Come

Living as a political exile in his desert hideaway east of the Jordan (*Lo-debar*, literally meaning a "barren place"), Mephibosheth seemed destined to live out his days in obscurity. However, as the distant rumbling sound of the horses of David's men drew nearer, he knew that they would soon descend on the compound. Since his dynasty was at odds with the new king, he must have thought his death was imminent when he was taken to Jerusalem to face David, his number one enemy. Surely this would be the last day of his life. Mephibosheth hated King David not only because of the overthrow of the line of Saul, but because of the accident that occurred during his flight into exile. His nurse had panicked and dropped him, rendering him a cripple for the rest of his life. In those days if you were not physically fit it was very hard to find work or be useful. David, no doubt, was a constant cause of cursing to Mephibosheth. He expected little mercy.

Fear Not

However, the first words David spoke to Mephibosheth were most unexpected. "Fear not," the king calmly declared. Instead of swiftly carrying out the inevitable execution David seemed to reach out in friendship. In a moment, all the evil preconceptions Mephibosheth held about David were swept away. His enemy was really his friend! Sadly, many people today have wrong preconceptions about God, seeing Him in similarly harsh terms: the angry One waiting to hurl a thunderbolt at anyone who steps out of line! Yet in reality, God wants to give us His friendship and love. He says to those paralysed by the wrong kind of religious teaching, "Fear not."

Excessive Favour

David greets Mephibosheth like a long lost son and staggers him with an awesome declaration. Instead of suffering at the hands of the king, he is granted quarters in the palace, given a permanent place at the king's table, and effectively adopted as one of the king's sons! What an amazing picture! You can imagine a banquet at David's palace: Tamar, David's daughter, known as one of the most beautiful women in Israel, Absalom, one of the most handsome young men in Israel, Solomon, to become one of the wisest men in the history of mankind, and Joab, the mightiest warrior in Israel. Then there would be the courtiers and servants dressed in finest array around the king's banqueting table. And there at the same table was the king's former enemy, Mephibosheth the cripple – though now he was on the same level, and had the same status, as everyone else. A day which seemed to begin so disastrously had suddenly seen him granted a permanent place of provision, status and blessing. The exiled outlaw now lived as one of the king's sons! Crippled Mephibosheth could never repay the debt to David; he could only enjoy the king's unbelievable generosity. No matter what you think of yourself, remember that by God's grace there is a place for you too at the King's table.

David's Desire to Bless

What was David's motive? He had a desire to bless the descendants of Jonathan. He wanted to do something beyond the normal; perhaps he wanted this man to be blessed so that everyone could see he was not the enemy of Saul's dynasty? God too wants to lavish us with His goodness, that He *"... might show the exceeding riches of His grace in His kindness toward us in Christ Jesus"* (Ephesians 2:4–10). He wants to show the world how exceedingly rich is His grace towards those who believe in Him. He wants to show the world what He is really like through us.

In Jonathan

David blessed Mephibosheth because he was in the line of Jonathan. David had made a covenant with Jonathan and his descendants. He wanted to fully express this now. Even though he didn't even know Mephibosheth, he wanted to bless him because he was "in Jonathan" and so was a recipient of the covenant he made. God too has a covenant, cut with His very blood, that subjects us to the most amazing blessing quite simply because we are "in Christ." God the Father wants to pour His goodness out on His Son. We are in Christ Jesus and so just as God the Father wants to bless His Son Christ Jesus, He wants to bless us. The New Testament is packed with all the promises of who we now are "in Christ", and all the promises of God are "yes" to every believer (2 Corinthians 1:20). In fact, Christ has chosen to share everything He has with us making us, *"heirs of God and joint heirs with Christ"* (Romans 8:17). Mephibosheth did nothing to deserve David's favour; this typifies God's grace to each of us which is completely unearned and undeserved.

Grace's Initiative

David took the initiative by sending his servants way across the Jordan to search for Mephibosheth. In the same way God took the initiative with us, taking the ultimate step of reconciliation: *"God demonstrates His own love toward us, in that while we were still sinners, Christ died for us"* (Romans 5:8). Jesus took the first step, laying down His life, with no guarantee that we would respond. Jesus said, *"the Son of Man has come to seek and to save that which was lost"* (Luke 19:10). He still earnestly seeks those who will receive the incredible provision of His grace. God's grace has taken an enormous step towards each and every person through the coming of Christ.

Beyond Forgiveness

Christ could have just given us a gospel of forgiveness. That would have been enough to get us to heaven. Even so, He went way beyond forgiveness; He gave us a gospel that brings us into all the privileges of being members of His family. It's like a man who catches a homeless thief stealing from his house. Forgiveness can be compared to letting the thief go without pressing charges, but grace is forgiving the thief and inviting him to live in the house as an adopted son! The gospel goes beyond what is necessary – forgiveness – and extends to give us all the privileges of sonship.

Please, Just Receive it!

This story is just a small glimpse into God's grace towards us. Just like Mephibosheth, we were once in exile, far from God's goodness, but He has taken the initiative and reached out to each one of us through Christ. Like the cripple Mephibosheth, we have nothing really to offer God; we can only receive His overwhelming grace towards us. We may feel completely unworthy that God should choose to express His love in such an excessive way. Just like Mephibosheth, we may want to earn God's goodness, but the first thing I believe the Father asks of us is to just receive it. Before entering into full-time ministry I was a school teacher. Some of the school children I used to teach would desperately seek to win my approval and attention by "over-doing" the instructions I gave them. I found that so difficult, at times I felt like saying, "Please, you don't have to try to impress me. I'll be the best school teacher I can be to you anyway!" Likewise, I'm sure at times our Father wants to say, "Please, please, just receive what I've done for you." When we insist on trying to earn God's love and approval we are actually trying to dilute what He has accomplished in us through Christ.

Submitting to Grace

Like Peter we may draw back when Christ wants to wash our feet, but without His cleansing we can't be clean. There is an inherent attitude in our hearts that struggles to just sit back and receive. Many have been brought up with the saying, "Nothing in life is free" and taught that *everything* has to be earned. Often our lives display a lack of confidence in God's grace and we struggle to simply accept our new position in Christ because we think, "Surely I must earn my righteousness?" But in doing so we seek to dilute God's grace which can never be added to by our works. As Paul states, *"And if by grace, then it is no longer of works; otherwise grace is no longer grace"* (Romans 11:6).

The Only Foundation

If we don't begin our Christian lives from a real understanding of grace then the foundation of our whole faith is faulty and will affect everything we do. As Paul so strongly made clear to the Ephesians, *"For by grace you have been saved through faith, and that not of yourselves; it is the gift of God, not of works, lest anyone should boast"* (Ephesians 2:8–9). Grace undergirds our faith. If we attempt to try to earn the Father's favour we into the same trap as many of the Jewish people in the New Testament, *"For they being ignorant of God's righteousness, and seeking to establish their own righteousness, have not submitted to the righteousness of God"* (Romans 10:3).

Often when I travel through countries in desperate need, I am utterly overwhelmed by the generosity of the people. At first I used to refuse their gifts of kindness, feeling it was inappropriate. One time a man in Cotonou, West Africa paid a significant sum of money to video our meetings and wanted to give the video to us. We tried to pay him knowing the effort he'd put in and were amazed by his response, "Don't steal my blessing!" he asserted. We knew all we could do was allow him to express his kindness to us, aware of the sacrifice he was making. I've since learnt how culturally offensive it can be *not* to receive a gift. Grace cuts into our human pride and self-sufficiency. It simply has to be received. We must lay aside our instinctive desire to *earn* and *deserve* things and truly submit to the provision Christ made at Calvary.

Chapter 2

Grace to the Prodigal

Luke 15:11–32

The Only Place Left to Go

In Luke 15 we see perhaps the New Testament's most elaborate example of God's incredible forgiveness and grace. The story begins with a young man asking for his inheritance *before* the death of his father – a shockingly selfish and greedy thing to do in any culture. In Israel however it was tantamount to saying, "I want you dead." It was perhaps the ultimate act of humiliation a son could inflict on his father; an insult that would normally have gone very deep in a cultural setting where forgiveness didn't come easily. Interestingly, the father in this story chooses to let his son go. He could have rightfully stopped him, but he chose to let him go and do his own thing. This reflects the heart of God. He doesn't want anyone in His house who in their heart of hearts, doesn't want to be there. God doesn't force us! He has given us freewill. Some legalistic believers try to force others to do certain things or behave in a certain way, but the way of grace is to look for a response of the heart, not merely outward conformity; Christ only wants willing followers.

The son journeyed to a far country, further emphasising his desire to be completely removed from his father and family. There, away from all constraints, he blew his inheritance in the worst kind of way with wild parties and prostitutes. Eventually famine hit the land and he hit rock bottom, forced into a job inconceivable for a Jewish boy: looking after pigs. As he plumbed the depths of despair, he began to pondered the unthinkable – to return in disgrace to his father. On the one hand, it was the last place he wanted to go, but on the other hand, probably the only place left that would have him. This is a paradox not dissimilar to the one faced by the average non-Christian today. The church can be a place of incredibly judgemental attitudes, yet it's also a place that offers God's astonishing forgiveness and grace. Considering what we have to offer our world, it's astonishing how graceless we must at times appear to non-Christians. One such person once said to a friend of mine, "The church! That would be the last place I would go to get help!" Philip Yancey poignantly expressed the dilemma, "I left the church because I saw such little grace; I came back because I could find it nowhere else."

Old Story, New Ending

So the prodigal son began his long journey home, agonising all the way, his feet bare, suffering every step of the way. He must have been kicking himself for his foolishness, rehearsing what he would say, and wondering if his father would ever want to see him again. Apparently in the Middle East, a story very similar to the one Jesus told, was widely known. The ending of course, was all too clear: the disobedient son would be punished, relegated to a life of servanthood and sent to the barn. Jesus however, must have utterly astonished His sinful listeners when He completely changed the ending! Far from punishing his son, the father acted in manner totally out of keeping with the culture of the day. While the boy was still a great way off, the father saw him. It implies that the father had been actively looking for him. Perhaps day by day he looked into the distance longing for his son's return. This expresses just a tiny bit of Christ's longing for the lost. He laid down His life for the world, and He longs for all to find salvation (2 Peter 3:9), not willing that anyone should miss it. The ageing father then proceeded to act in a highly undignified manner for such a patriarchal society: he *ran* to greet his son. Normally an occasion of this kind would call for an austere display of authority, but this father just couldn't hide his delight! Coming to his son, there was no rebuke or inquisition, but rather a heartfelt hug and kiss, the son's repentance being clearly obvious. It's at times distressing to compare the desire of the church for the lost with that of this father. I remember sitting in one meeting where a large number of young people made very public turning to Christ. A wife of one of the pastors turned around and said, "Oh no, how are we going to do all this counselling!" Perhaps if our hearts were filled with a little more desire for the lost, Christ might be more inclined to lead them to us!

Total Reinstatement

The father in Jesus' story didn't just stop at an emotional greeting. Oh no, he was far too excited to do that! The father, heartbroken at seeing his son dressed in rags, had the best robe brought out and put it on him. The family's ultimate designer outfit. What a contrast. The young man must have been completely caught off guard by his father's amazing generosity. His plan seems to have been to work his way back into his father's favour, so he wasn't prepared for this. On his return he declared, *"Father, I have sinned against heaven and in your sight, and am no longer worthy to be called your son"* (Luke 15:21). It's interesting that he used the phrase "no longer worthy." It seems that before his fall into sin, he believed that he was worthy! But, according to his reasoning, he thought the way back to his father must be through "work". *"Make me like one of your hired servants"* (Luke 15:19), he said. Like so many Christians, we think we can work our way into favour, rather than simply receiving God's undeserved goodness. What a glorious surprise for the son to find that his father completely reinstated his sonship with full privileges. He hoped for forgiveness and a life as a servant, but came to a wonderful realisation of how amazing grace could be.

Now the father really was on a roll! "Put a ring on his hand," he declared. The ring would have been the family signet ring, giving the owner the right to represent the family. Effectively the father was saying, "I receive you back as my son. No more grovelling. I fully reinstate you to all the privileges of sonship." In the same way, every blessing in Christ is given from the moment we are His. The blessings are so wonderful they take more than a lifetime to truly discover and understand.

Next the father had some proper shoes brought out, to cover what were probably damaged and scarred feet from the trip home. He then turned the whole household upside down declaring, "Bring the fatted calf here and kill it, and let us eat and be merry." The calf specially fattened for an important occasion, was about to enter its destiny! Everyone had to down tools, come in from the fields and celebrate. In that part of the world, such celebrations could go on for days! Again this story is just a pale reflection of what happens in heaven, where there is an explosion of joy every time someone comes back to the Father.

Catching the Father's Heart?

The amazingly gracious attitude of the father in Jesus' parable stands in stark contrast to many religious attitudes today. How do our hearts compare? Have we truly caught the Father's heartbeat for the lost? Do we still share the Father's joy over every life that turns to Him? Have we lost something of our compassion in the busyness of church life? Can you grasp how incredible the gospel really is, not just in terms of forgiveness, but because it invites us to be a member of Christ's royal family, along with all the privileges that brings? Have you perhaps lost sight of how incredibly gracious God has been in saving you?

Although the ongoing process of sanctification that follows our conversion is an important and necessary part of our becoming Christlike, in the eyes of the Father at the moment of our commitment to Christ, the key foundation is already in place. At the very moment of turning to Christ, the former sinner has immediately crossed from darkness to light, from a destiny of destruction to eternal life, from having the identity of a sinner, to that of a saint, from the control of Satan to being under the Lordship of Christ as a son of God. At that moment the very righteousness of God is imparted and that person is fully justified and declared holy. Working all that out and our gradual conformity into the image of Christ will take a lifetime, but the position and privileges are already in place. This certainly explains to me why heaven is so much more excited over one sinner who turns to Christ, than 99 of us who seem to be doing fine!

At times we are so concerned that people will move on into the sanctification process each new believer must go through, that we rob ourselves of the enjoyment of witnessing the sheer joy to be found in their salvation and new position in Christ. It is so easy to lose sight of the sense of wonder we have for the overwhelming grace God's shows to each new believer. The religious leaders of the day were very upset at how Jesus could just forgive hopeless sinners. There just wasn't any room for it in their dry legalistic approach to God. Grace was simply just not a part of their theology.

The Priority of Jesus

For Jesus, modelling God's grace was a priority. In Matthew chapter 9 we read:

"Now it happened, as Jesus sat at the table in the house, that behold, many tax collectors and sinners came and sat down with Him and His disciples. And when the Pharisees saw it, they said to His disciples, 'Why does your Teacher eat with tax collectors and sinners?' When Jesus heard that, He said to them, 'Those who are well have no need of a physician, but those who are sick. But go and learn what this means: "I desire mercy and not sacrifice." For I did not come to call the righteous, but sinners, to repentance.'"

(Matthew 9:10–13)

Jesus' words could be paraphrased, "I want a people who minister My mercy rather than being selfishly concerned with mere outward rules and regulations. I'm right where I'm meant to be, with the spiritually sick."

True Holiness

Today in the church we are beginning to see the restoration of an emphasis on holiness, but there is perhaps a danger of over-emphasising the avoidance of sins of commission: drunkenness, lying, etc., rather than sins of omission – what we're neglecting to do. The popular modern catchphrase, "What would Jesus do?" is often followed by a mental list of things He *didn't* do, rather then the positive things He *did* do!

Jesus didn't defensively spend His time worrying about losing His sanctification, but rather He threw Himself into the Father's mission of reaching sinners. His holiness took

Him to some of the most unholy people of the day, yet He never once lost the sanctity of His inward separation to the Father. Ed Silvoso summed the ultimate end of holiness up so well, "If the only thing God wanted from us was to be holy, then we might as well drop dead right now and be with God in heaven. We are going to be more holy there than any place else!" Perhaps the main reason for inner holiness is that we remain clean and undiluted in order to fulfil our mission here on earth, rather than escape from it. We can look at holiness negatively, rather than positively as a catalyst that propels us into our destiny in Christ. T.L. Osborn summarises this aspect of holiness so well by declaring, "The holiest experience you can have with Christ is to lead a person to Christ." He also warns, "We go from our holy home to our holy pew and miss all the holy things between: lifting up the fallen sinners to Christ." Real holiness means we will hold to the same holy attitudes and actions of Christ and His desire to lift others.

Chapter 3

The Elder Brother Problem

An Understandable Reaction?

The elder brother of the prodigal son in Jesus' parable had serious problems with his father's outpouring of grace upon his wayward son, and didn't hold back from saying so. This elder brother outwardly seemed so right and in the original version of the story would have been hailed as the good and upright son. But, from the perspective of grace he falls completely short. There's probably something in us all that sympathizes with him. He had been loyal and faithful in serving his father. He had seen his brother utterly insult his father and then proceed to blow everything in the worst possible way with parties and prostitutes. His family has been shamed and disgraced and so there is a sense of justice about his cause. How could his father be so stupid? How could he respond in such an excessive way? Grace takes a lot of understanding!

My Righteousness

The elder brother knew so little about the heart of his father and, it seems, little knowledge of his own predicament. In his discourse to his father he reveals how he really sees himself: *"All these years I've been **slaving** for you and never disobeyed your orders"* (Luke 15:29 NIV). He appealed to his own righteousness. He felt his years of service surely meant he deserved something. So different from the son who simply said, *"I have sinned against heaven and against you. I am no longer worthy to be called your son"* (Luke 15:18–19).

I Want Justice!

Today I sometimes hear Christians say, "I want justice!" However if God truly gave us His justice outside of grace, how would we stand? If God were to appear to each of us in all His awesome holiness and reveal every area in us that is displeasing in His sight, how would we cope? Isaiah was a righteous and powerful prophet to Israel, however when the king of glory revealed Himself He cried out,

> *"Woe is me, for I am undone!*
> *Because I am a man of unclean lips,*
> *And I dwell in the midst of a people of unclean lips."*
> (Isaiah 6:5)

Thankfully for all of us God normally deals with us one issue at a time, rather than completely overwhelming us with all our faults at once. Sanctification is a process that takes a lifetime.

The Grace Necessity

Our righteousness, however wonderful it may look from our perspective, just doesn't stand up in the sight of a holy God! The elder brother in comparing himself with his sinful brother missed it completely. When we compare our righteousness or holiness to that of others, we miss it completely too! The only true comparison can be with God Himself, to whom we all fall utterly short. This brother needed the grace of the father just as much as his brother. As James so clearly states, *"For whoever shall keep the whole law, and yet stumble in one point, he is guilty of all"* (James 2:10). Whether we feel we've scored 99% or 1% on our righteousness chart, we've all failed! The pass mark is 100% and only Jesus achieved that.

Didn't Know the Father's Goodness

Interestingly the elder brother hadn't understood how generous his father really was. He complained after all his hard work, *"You never gave me a young goat, that I might make merry with my friends"* (Luke 15:29). He must have been surprised by the father's response, *"Son, you are always with me, and all that I have is yours"* (Luke 15:31). In other words, "You too could have had anything that was in the house, but you never asked!" Despite the fact that the elder brother had lived with his father all those years, he still seemed distant from his heart and goodness. It is a tragedy when we fail to draw on our Father's generosity and effectively "block" others around us from being blessed. As Jesus charged the religious of His day: *"You neither go in yourselves, nor do you allow those who are entering to go in"* (Matthew 23:13). They refused to accept the grace and forgiveness Jesus brought, and then tried to stop others receiving it too! There's something in human nature that determines, "If I can't have it, why should you?" Like many Christians today, the elder brother, in all his faithful service had somehow, even while living in the same house, become alienated from his father. When the prodigal comes home and immediately receives a blessing from his father, it triggers a swift reaction in his elder brother. Sometimes when a brand new Christian comes under tremendous blessings from the Father, it's sad to see how "mature" Christians react.

We have a duty to catch the utter goodness of our heavenly Father, so our lives can truly radiate it to everyone around us. I'm always mildly amused by the sticker, "Don't follow me, follow Jesus." The obvious problem for the unbeliever is, "Where is Jesus?" Right now we're all He has now to reveal Himself through. He wants to hold each one of us up to a fallen world and say, "Look at what I can do with a life that's given over to Me." Jesus radically declared, *"You are the light of the world. A city that is set on a hill cannot be hidden. Nor do they light a lamp and put it under a basket, but on a lampstand, and it gives light to all who are in the house. Let your light so shine before men ... "* (Matthew 5:14–16). As we know the outpouring of God's grace in our hearts, so we can bless those around us by "letting our light shine before men." Sadly the elder brother, as with all those who depend on their self-righteousness, was a poor advertisement for the goodness of his father.

Seeing Others by Knowing Ourselves

There is something here for all of us who are immersed in service for God. It's so easy for us to slip into self-righteousness, to begin to judge those who haven't got it together as we have. Once a preacher was returning to his hotel room in a lift after an awesome move of God in a meeting he just preached at, when three drunks got in. Appalled at their behaviour he inwardly complained as to why the hotel management allowed this kind of thing to go on when the Holy Spirit spoke to him saying, "The only difference between them and you is Me!" Do we miss God's heart when incorrigible sinners come to God and immediately find His total acceptance and blessing? Shouldn't they earn it a bit? In my own walk with Christ seeing how new believers come so quickly into God's blessing these days can be such a challenge! Considering how long it took me it doesn't seem fair! But then God is so gracious.

How Do We Really Compare?

We so often fall down by our comparisons. We might think, "I'm basically good. Much better then some of my other

Christian friends." We may even begin to believe that's how God must see us! But the truth is, no matter how progressive our sanctification process may be, we still need God's grace in order to stand before Him. Every once in a while it is good to re-evaluate how we stand before God – by fulfilling various laws or by grace? By His provision or ours? By the work of the flesh or the Spirit? By faith or works? It is good to regularly encounter again the "reformation" truth that our standing in God is purely by faith!

It's easy to become critical of other believers or other churches, but when we look at ourselves from the viewpoint of a holy God, suddenly everything is put into perspective. Besides, how can we be so critical, when God has been so gracious? When we see how gracious He is to us, we can only become more gracious to others.

In Proverbs 6:16–19 there is a list of things that God hates. Hate number one is extremely surprising: "A proud look" – that patronising little look of superiority that we can so easily succumb to. It's not really a sin we preach against much! But to the Father who has given so much grace to each one of us, it's extremely disappointing. It's what stirred Jesus against the Pharisees and sadly it's a sin that can often be present in the body of Christ today. What gives us the right to look down on anyone! Who knows where we all would be were it not for Christ's grace given to us?

Chapter 4

Have We Really Received the Good News?

Possessing the Message

Sometimes, looking around the average Bible-believing church one might be forgiven for asking, "Where is the good news here?" One preacher summed it up by saying, "The problem is this, Jesus was good news, but most Christians seem to be bad news!" Somehow we seem to have lost sight of how *good* our message really is. We act as if we're living in poverty, when really we're sitting on top of a gold mine. Often when I teach on evangelism the first question I ask is, "In your heart of hearts, do you really know the good news?" By "know" I'm referring to a deep inward conviction. Having found Christ in salvation God wants us to walk freely before Him. Condemnation should not be gripping us as it so often does. Of course the

Holy Spirit will come with His conviction when we mess up, but never condemnation. Conviction brings us to repentance; condemnation drags us down, causing a dark cloud to overshadow our walk with Christ, resulting in a perpetual sense of guilt. Gradually we can begin to feel we're falling short of even our own sense of right and wrong, and we nose dive into despondency. In time the enemy catches us in his net. We're no longer walking in freedom, enjoying Christ's abundant grace towards us, but slipping into terminal despair. The very people Christ is seeking to demonstrate His goodness through, can become those who look the most hopeless. We can't even sin happily any more! But Christ wants us to know in our hearts that we're forgiven, even though we fall short in different ways at times. His grace is unending, despite the fact that we may, at times, fall short of God's standards, we can know with absolute certainty that His grace still enables us to stand before Him. Yes of course we must keep short accounts with Him and confess our sins as the Holy Spirit convicts us, but underneath it all the Father wants us to know we are covered by His undeserved grace. The grace of God is ours to enjoy all the way through our process of growth and development, not just at its completion. The gospel literally means, "the good news." Not just for the moment of salvation, but good news for the rest of our lives. Evangelism begins when we possess the message we're seeking to share. As Peter said to the cripple, *"Such as I have give I thee ... "* (Acts 3:6 KJV). Ultimately we can only effectively give away what we have ourselves received and continue to live in.

Back to the Cross

Imagine you wrecked my car and sheepishly came to tell me what you'd done and I said, "Oh well, have my house too!" You'd be astonished I'm sure. You may well question my sanity! However, God not only forgives us for wrecking our lives, He freely bestows the enormous privilege of being a part of His house as sons! The gospel of grace is more than just Christ writing off our un-payable bad debt, it is Christ further offering us free access to every privilege of His household! It wipes out the negative and gives the outrageous blessing of becoming a child of God. Often when we hear about the overwhelming generosity of God's grace, something within us seems to shrink back; it seems so unreal to our earning-based mindset. How can all this debt just be written off and all this abundance just be poured upon us? How can all this really be ours for free? It doesn't make sense! Really grace only makes sense when we go back time and time again to where it was purchased. The gospel is free, but it cost Christ everything. It's only as we focus once again on the cross that we can see clearly that total justice has indeed been done. The grace of God is not some frivolous freebee, but an awesome treasure purchased at the greatest possible expense. It is only as we consider God's Son dying in utter agony for the sins of our world, that grace makes any sense. What to the Pharisees was a blasphemous and seemingly causal bestowing of forgiveness by Jesus on those who asked for it, was in fact an act done in the full knowledge that every single one of those sins would have to be tortuously paid for by the most gruesome death known to man.

In highlighting the awesome benefits of grace, we should never move away from the overwhelming price it cost. Martyn Lloyd-Jones described the cross as, "the very heart of the gospel." Everything before the cross points to it and everything we have after the cross stems from it. No matter how advanced our teaching has become it's in the provision of the cross that the whole Christian life is rooted. The cross stands as the fountain of life, the place where God's grace began and from where the benefits outlined continue. In all our focus on grace we should never move away from its precious source.

Living in the Goodness of the Cross

When Christ died He purchased not only our redemption from sin but also opened up to us all the benefits of our new identity in Him. The privilege of walking and coming before Him with confidence and freedom, truly knowing our sins are forever dealt with, and wonderful abundant life has been opened up to us. He came to *"proclaim liberty to the captives"* (Luke 4:18). Imagine buying someone a gift and them refusing to receive it. You would want to know why! It must hurt the Lord so much when His children don't enter into all that He purchased. What a waste! When we believe and receive all the benefits of the cross it must delight the Lord so much, seeing His most precious gift honoured and enjoyed. He truly does have pleasure in the prosperity of His servants (Psalm 35:27).

Chapter 5

Grace-filled Evangelism

*"Let your speech always be with grace,
seasoned with salt, that you may know
how you ought to answer each one."*
(Colossians 4:6)

Two Beggars

Somehow here in the West the non-Christian world is not
hearing the gospel of grace. Many understand something of
the outworking of the Christian life, but know little of its
actual foundation. Often they know a lot about what the
church is *against*, but not much about the positive message
it proclaims. Perhaps as we have struggled to understand the
grace-basis to our faith, this has affected how we
communicate the gospel to others.

Our speech to non-Christians, especially when trying to
communicate the gospel, is not always delivered "with
grace" as Paul said it should be. The way some Christians
speak actually attracts a defensive response, yet grace-filled
words have a disarming effect. But what is the point of

winning an argument but losing the person? Charles
Spurgeon described evangelism as, "One beggar telling
another beggar where the bread is." This wonderful
description highlights two things: firstly there is nothing
innately better about one beggar than the other, just that
one has found the bread source. Secondly it shows that the
"beggar" isn't meant to feel superior to his colleague. He is
merely fulfilling a reasonable social responsibility in letting
the other suffering beggar know how to stay alive.
Sometimes as we "declare the Word of God" we can come
across as though we are talking down to people. People read
our hearts and as a result reject our message. They
intuitively pick up our sense of superiority and feel
patronised. In contrast, ordinary people were drawn to Jesus
because of His love and willingness to take accept them as
they were. A question I grapple with regularly with is, "Why
were sinners so attracted to Jesus and yet stay away in their
droves from church?" Perhaps one key is our need to freshly
understand God's grace.

What Was Jesus Known For?

> *"The Son of Man has come eating and drinking, and
> you say, 'Look, a glutton and a winebibber, a friend of
> tax collectors and sinners!'"* (Luke 7:34)

Perhaps the greatest criticism Jesus' actions received
concerned His continual habit of hanging out with the
wrong kind of people! It just didn't seem to add up, a Holy
man claiming to be the Messiah spending so much time

with the dregs of society. The Pharisees couldn't understand Jesus' purpose and mission. When the sinful woman poured the worship of her tears upon the feet of Jesus, they criticised Him among themselves, saying, *"This Man, if He were a prophet, would know who and what manner of woman this is who is touching Him, for she is a sinner"* (Luke 7:39). Throughout His ministry Jesus had to stress time and time again that reaching "the sinner" was His purpose.

If you talk to a number of Christian leaders about what their church has ever been persecuted for, you will often receive a reply that they came under pressure because they made a stand over some moral issue. As "salt" in the world, there are of course times when the church should and must speak out. But, I've never once heard of a church being persecuted for the actions they persecuted Jesus for – spending too much time with sinners! There were enormous moral, political and ethical faults in the Roman Empire that Jesus could have attacked, but He did not choose to make any of these the focus of His mission. The only place He really went beserk, was not over the sin of the non-religious, but when the religious leaders were abusing His Father's house through unrighteous trade!

So, of course the church should at times protest and speak into our society, but is this the priority of the church in the light of the mission that Christ has for us? Why is the church chiefly known for what it's *against* rather than what it's *for*? Is the gospel of grace clearly being heard through us?

Chapter 6

Grace-filled Eyes

Grace-Touched People Become Gracious

Truly embracing the grace of God extended towards us should change how we view others. As we are changed by God's grace we become *more* gracious. If we view God as judgemental and fundamentally negative, that in turn will affect how we see others. But as we receive the grace of God, we're indebted to pass it on to others. "Freely you have received, freely give," Jesus said. Knowing God's amazing grace in our hearts changes the basis of how we minister and act towards others. A clear sign that we're struggling to embrace God's grace is that we become ungracious and overcritical of others!

Same Church, Two Totally Different Views

Having, or not having, grace-filled eyes affects our view of others to such an extent that it is possible to hold two

completely different views of the same person/people,
depending on the state of our own heart. Look at this
interesting statement in Acts: chapter 15 records of the
church in Antioch that, *"certain men came down from
Judea and taught the brethren, 'Unless you are circumcised
according to the custom of Moses, you cannot be saved'"*
(Acts 15:1). Here was the first Gentile church, multiracial,
growing, prospering, having already sent out a mission
team and planted other churches. A wonderful picture
of what the church should be like. Well not to the
legalists! Note the phrase *"certain men came down ... "*
In other words they were not *sent* and did not represent
the Jerusalem church. Often it's the self-appointed and
unaccountable who cause the most problems in the body
of Christ. To these "certain men" the whole church in
Antioch was not even saved yet! A nearly unbelievable
conclusion considering how the Holy Spirit was moving
among them and the impact of their first mission. These
men just couldn't see past their doctrinal dogmas to grasp
God's evident grace upon this group. Effectively their
legalistic view was, unless it's done our way it can't be
God!

He Saw the Grace of God

However, we read that, *"When he [Barnabas] came and had
seen the grace of God, he was glad, and encouraged them all
that with purpose of heart they should continue with the
Lord. For he was a good man, full of the Holy Spirit and of
faith"* (Acts 11:22–24).

Barnabas had a completely different view of the same church! He saw God's grace upon them and encouraged them. Yes, they were totally different from his home church in Jerusalem, but his heart was big enough to see past the differences to God's grace. In fact Barnabas seems to have made this a habit which is probably why the Jerusalem leaders entrusted him with such a sensitive task as checking up on the first Gentile church. He was the first to see that former enemy number one, Paul, had genuinely found Christ (Acts 9:27) and put his reputation on the line in support of him. Paul later records, *"and when James, Cephas, and John, who seemed to be pillars, perceived the grace that had been given to me, they gave me and Barnabas the right hand of fellowship"* (Galatians 2:9). Paul remained indebted to Barnabas' ability to help him through those sensitive early days following his conversion. Barnabas was a grace spotter. He didn't allow his former prejudice or preconceived ideas to stop him recognising God's grace at work in others. His faith-filled heart saw that God's grace extended far wider than his own background and customs. He was a pioneer who helped the Jerusalem church understand and embrace their new Gentile brethren. He then demonstrated one of the most natural fruits of grace; he encouraged these new Gentile believers. There is rarely any encouragement from those still bound in legalism. Looking back it's also a relief that the Council that resulted from this dispute in Jerusalem settled the matter of the Mosaic Law once and for all (Acts 15:22) by concluding that the Gentile believers were not subject to it. One wonders how many men would respond to an evangelistic appeal if circumcision were a requirement of salvation!

Paul's Incredible View of the Corinthians

*"To the church of God which is at Corinth, to those who are sanctified in Christ Jesus, called **to be** saints . . ."*

(1 Corinthians 1:2)

*"I thank my God always concerning you for the grace of God which was given to you by Christ Jesus, that you were enriched in everything by Him in all utterance and all knowledge, even as the testimony of Christ was confirmed in you, so that you come short in no gift, eagerly waiting for the revelation of our Lord Jesus Christ, who will also confirm you to the end, **that you may be** blameless in the day of our Lord Jesus Christ. God **is** faithful, by whom you were called into the fellowship of His Son, Jesus Christ our Lord."*

(1 Corinthians 1:4–9)

Paul's opening comments to probably the most carnal church in the New Testament are nothing short of staggering! Considering Paul was to go on and confront an openly incestuous relationship, drunkenness at the Lord's table and blatant personality sectarianism, it is amazing his letter begins, *"to those who are sanctified in Christ Jesus."* An amazing statement of faith! Undoubtedly Paul had to choose to view this unruly church through grace-filled eyes. He chose to see them in Christ, from Christ's perspective, in their redeemed state, before he began to focus on how they could bring their behaviour more in line with their position! If I were writing to this church I'm not sure I would have begun so positively! Paul clearly had trained himself to see with the eyes of faith. His attitude remains really quite astonishing, *"I thank my God always concerning you for the grace of God which was given to you by Christ Jesus ... "* He thanked God always for the grace given to them. There is such a key lesson here for us all, especially those involved in pastoral ministry. Even with the horrific depths of carnality the Corinthians had sunk to, he still always thanked God for them, acknowledging the grace Christ had given to this church. He even expressed his confidence, *"that you may be blameless in the day of our Lord Jesus Christ. God is faithful ... "* Paul here exhibits incredible leadership, having unbelievable faith for this seriously sinful church. Whether it is concerning our church or our own family, Christ wants us to have His perspective of His people. Before we just focus on the outward failings, He wants to give a revelation of how He sees people in His grace. We truly need to see His people in the light of His grace.

Which Is More Powerful, Adam's Sin or Christ's Redemption?

*"Therefore, as through one man's offence **judgment** came to all men, resulting in condemnation, even so through one Man's righteous act **the free gift came** to all men, resulting in justification of life. For as by one*

> *man's disobedience many were made sinners, so also by*
> *one Man's obedience many will be made righteous."*
>
> (Romans 5:18–19)

This passage begs the question, "What is more powerful, Adam's sin or the power of Christ's redemption?" As unbelievers Scripture tells us we were born in Adam and as a result of his sin, we were by nature born as sinners (Ephesians 2:3). The negative is true, but the positive much more so. As believers we are now "in Christ" and are now in the same way subject to all the benefits of His obedience: *"For as by one man's disobedience many were made sinners, so also by one Man's obedience many will be made righteous."* Listening to many Christians you would think Adam's sin had greater power than Christ's redemption! However, His redemption is total and complete; we not only have a new nature but are now automatically credited with His righteousness and therefore His righteous position. As we look at ourselves and others we need to ask God for a revelation to see as He sees, rather than just seeing the outward failings. I will never forget the time when the Holy Spirit clearly spoke deep into my spirit, "I have imparted to you My righteousness." Suddenly I was overwhelmed with a real sense that unworthy little me could stand before God, men and even Satan himself, totally complete in His righteousness. What an awesome relief I felt, no more striving to try and make myself "good enough". At that moment I truly entered a "rest of faith" where I ended my fleshly attempts to be OK with God and fully and completely trusted in His grace. It was He who made me OK now. What's more I've lived so much more righteously ever since!

Focusing on God's Grace

Having been privileged to preach in nearly twenty different nations it's been truly amazing to observe how diverse the body of Christ really is. The different emphases and insights have enriched me and broadened my understanding of the Father. On the other hand though it's been saddening at times to see how narrow-minded the church can be. The most extreme requirements have been added to the gospel. In one country if you drink any alcohol you can't be saved, in another if you're unwilling to sip the local wine with the pastor you're seen as being offensive. In one church women wearing make-up means "they're going straight to hell," in another if the women aren't dressed to the nines they're compromising the excellence of God!

A Strange People

We really are a very funny bunch! I remember something that happened on a mission trip when we gave an altar call in a rural village. The people responded well and duly came forward to receive Christ. However, just before the preacher was about to lead them in the sinner's prayer the local leader asked him to wait. The local women then scuttled into the surrounding buildings grabbing every available cloth and rag. They then proceeded to cover the heads of every woman that had come forward so that God would accept them as they prayed the sinner's prayer! Having laughed with everyone at the ridiculousness of the sight I was naturally concerned in my heart. I sensed the need to pray and the

Lord showed me that this particular group was the one that God had graced to reach this area and that I was not to take the matter up, after all in a few days we would be on the plane home. Even with their strong legalistic tendencies they were the people God had graced to reach that community.

To All of His Body

"To each one of us grace was given ... " (Ephesians 4:7)

The above examples reflect some of the extremes in Christ's body. We can laugh at how ridiculous we can be. But knowing God's grace can challenge all of us on our core attitudes to others in the body of Christ. Do we really see that God has graced all of His body with something unique which can bring great blessing to us? It so easy to ignore or criticise from a distance, other parts of the body that haven't seen our "revelation". It is much less complicated to just fellowship with those who believe and practise as we do. They affirm our convictions, but rarely challenge us to see the outworking of God's grace on a broader basis. It's so easy to throw grenades at those who haven't understood as we have, when we don't have to work through our beliefs with them in relationship. The Father, just in my lifetime, has revealed afresh many truths that have in the past been neglected or ignored: commitment to discipleship, moving in faith, the charismatic move, restoration of the church, the prophetic, signs and wonders, moves of refreshing, a fresh call to holiness etc. All these have played a significant part in shaping church as we know it today. The danger comes when having experienced God's presence and grace in our own particular way, we ignore, or even fight against what Christ is trying to add to us through other parts of His body. Sometimes our understanding of the way in which God has graced us, becomes a barrier to receiving something new the Lord is trying to show us.

Same Mountain, Different View

I've heard it said, "No one ministry is balanced, the balance is in the body." The prophet isn't balanced by himself – he needs the other members of the fivefold ministry to keep the overall ministry to the church in right order. The same is true for all the ministries. I believe as the church comes more and more into maturity we will finally grasp just how much we really need each other! God in His mercy hasn't given any one individual or group everything! If you were to put five people on different sides of a mountain and ask them to draw what they see, they would all draw something different. Is one wrong? Of course not, they're all drawing the same mountain from the viewpoint they've been given. The Father has graced each ministry with a certain revelation of Himself, so that when we come to together, we begin to see the whole picture.

No Compromise!

Some assert that by mixing too much with those from outside their group they are in danger of "compromising" their revelation or message. However, by having healthy fellowship with those who may question and be initially less receptive, we are drawing the wider body into something new, rather then just, "getting on with it" only with those who agree with us. The pioneer may at times have to tread a lonely path of criticism and misunderstanding, but more often than not the revelation will eventually be absorbed into the wider body, as relationships of love are maintained. In fact, by fellowshipping exclusively with those we are in agreement with, we are compromising the full breadth of Christ's body and His commandment to truly love all of His people. Some say, "I can't compromise my beliefs" and yet by their actions they totally compromise the command of Jesus to love all of His disciples. It's easier to be exclusive, but ultimately we're the one's missing out, no matter how powerful our revelation is. By fellowshipping and honouring God's grace in other lives and churches, we are not compromising the truth that we know, but enabling it to spread more widely. There should be no compromise in our corporate understanding of God's grace to all of His body. We could instead become modern day grace-spotters like Barnabas, doing all we can to find God's grace in other parts of His body. Lyndon Bowring, the Chairman of Care, once spoke to me of his desire to actively view everyone from this perspective: "What of Jesus can I see in this person." It is so important to do this in our approach to others. I can remember two people sharing with me their opinions about a meeting we were all attending. One person complained at its length, the style of worship and the outfit the preacher was wearing. The other revealed the impact the meeting had on his walk with God and explained that it had drawn Him so much closer to Jesus. Perhaps if we actively look for that which God has graced a ministry with, we will find it. If we actively look for faults in others they are not normally hard to find! It's our approach that is the key.

Chapter 7

I Am What I Am, by God's Grace

"Having then gifts differing according to the grace that is given to us, let us use them."
(Romans 12:6)

Not Rewards

It's one thing to see that our salvation is by grace; however grace goes much deeper than that. Often there can be the tendency to slip back into old ways of viewing ourselves – especially in the area of our ministry to the body of Christ. "Look what my prayers have done ... wasn't that a powerful prophecy ... " etc. Whilst the Bible clearly teaches us to invest and use the talents God has given us, there should be a real appreciation that they are given as an act of His grace. A gift is after all, a gift, not a reward for achievement. Each of the fivefold ministries is a *grace* from the ascended Lord, *"to each one of us grace was given*

according to the measure of Christ's gift" (Ephesians 4:7).
Our ministries are grace gifts from Christ to bless His body,
not trophies to boast over. Why boast about something we
haven't earned?

"My God Don't Make No Junk"

Again Paul stresses grace in the list of "motivation" gifts
listed in Romans, stating that we have *". . . gifts differing
according to the grace that is given to us"* (Romans 12:6).
Paul says that even our underlying motivations are grace
gifts from God, pulling us in the direction of our destiny. At
times our individual ministries can be unduly influenced by
the humanistic teaching that so saturates our modern
culture. How many times have we heard statements such as,
"You can do anything if you set your mind to it"? Because
of this type of thinking, our lives and ministries can become
driven by a philosophy of "If they can do it, so can I." As a
result we may end up blindly copying others who we
perceive as "successful", thinking that this or that technique
will bring the same success to us. Of course we can learn,
and at times develop, from looking at those God has blessed,
however, the truth is a lot more exciting. You are not meant
to be someone else's copy, God made you an original. God
created you totally unique and special, and gave you a
purpose that only you can fulfil. Paul included you in his
statement when we said of all believers, *"We are God's
workmanship, created in Christ Jesus to do good works,
which God prepared in advance for us to do"* (Ephesians
2:10 NIV).

A friend in Malaysia used to laugh so much at the Rolex wristwatch salesman who would say, "Genuine copy sir!" God is not looking for second rate copies; He has prepared from the foundation of the earth a special and significant work for you to do. Copies are never as good as the originals, and God never intended you to be anything less than His originally-designed blessing to the world! As one preacher of the Deep South once declared, "My God don't make no junk." He only makes the best. You are unique to God and precious, irrespective of the circumstances in which you were born. God is the Master Craftsman. God's destiny and purpose on your life is a grace He gave just to you! What is even more releasing is the fact that He has graced you with the ability to do everything He's called you to do. Of course we need to use and develop our grace gifts in order for them to become more and more effective, but all the while remaining aware that, *"It is God who works in you both to will and to do for His good pleasure"* (Philippians 2:13).

What's Growing Within?

God's will is revealed in us as we allow Him to work His desires and purposes deep into our hearts. As we develop spiritually, that purpose, gift and call He has graced us will begin to grow. Our call is an inward discovery, not a choice. What fills your heart with compassion? The poor, the unreached, the sick, orphans, the untaught? What makes you angry? Injustice, the church in disrepair? Such deep inner works of the Holy Spirit in our hearts are normally the keys to the work God is graciously calling us into. A God-graced call is rarely something totally external. It comes from the stirrings deep within and is often confirmed by those around us. This was how Paul's ministry was finally recognized by the leaders in Jerusalem: *"And when James, Cephas, and John, who seemed to be pillars, perceived the grace that had been given to me ... "* (Galatians 2:9). When it's truly Him there is a sense of peace and a natural, but supernatural, flow from within. There is a sense of His grace.

No Need to Compete

As we realise that God determines our true destiny and gifting, we can settle secure in our own uniqueness and special-ness to God. There is no longer any need for competition with others because we realise others' grace is not necessarily our grace. Instead of feeling threatened we can honour and receive the ministry and blessing others can bring to us. In other words by knowing our giftings are given to us by His grace, the striving and competitiveness can be taken out of God's work. I don't have to be like anyone else and I'm free to be me! If the whole body of Christ could truly come to terms with God's grace in this area we could flow together so much more effectively and perhaps stop wasting time and energy trying to be something God never created us to be. None of us will ever be graced with everything, we need each other. Someone once said, "The only person on their own in the New Testament was in jail!" As the fivefold ministry flows together we will truly come to the *"unity of the faith and of the knowledge of the Son of God, to a perfect man, to the measure of the stature of the fullness of Christ; that we should no longer be children, tossed to and fro and carried about with every wind of doctrine"* (Ephesians 4:12–14). The wholeness of the body will develop not only as we flow where we are graced, but also as we allow others to develop us though their graced ministries.

An Identity in Grace

"But by the grace of God I am what I am."
(1 Corinthians 15:10)

In this amazing statement, Paul is saying that everything we are, we are by God's grace. Paul saw his whole life and personality was as a result of God's grace. In fact some might say this was Paul's argument to the Corinthian church as it struggled to accept him, "I am what I am by God's grace." In other words please accept me with all my Pauline tendencies, as I'm a product of God's grace! His personality, talents and identity were all wrapped up in God's grace. Paul was certainly a strong personality and at times might appear a "self-made man," but throughout his epistles he makes it abundantly clear that whatever he is or will become is by God's grace to him. He regularly repeats his clear understanding that his calling and identity is a work of grace:

"Through Him we have received grace and apostleship."
(Romans 1:5)

"According to the grace of God which was given to me, as a wise master builder I have laid the foundation."
(1 Corinthians 3:10)

"I became a minister according to the gift of the grace of God given to me."
(Ephesians 3:7)

Paul's Ministry

Paul as a former persecutor of the church knew so well he had been graced in a special way to be who he was and to carry out the ministry he had. This flies in the face in many of the implied admonitions today: "I got where I am today by sheer hard work" etc. Yet, if we allow ourselves to think like this, there is a real danger that we will begin to think that the ministry *belongs* to us. John Wimber once said humorously/seriously that the Holy Spirit spoke to him one day saying, "When you've finished your ministry I'll give you mine!" Ultimately when we finally stand before the Lord surely we won't be saying to Him, "Look what I did for you." A more likely statement would be, "Look what You did through me!" And Paul again in the context of the grace on his life, cautions us here, *"For I say, through the grace given to me, to everyone who is among you, not to think of himself more highly than he ought to think, but to think soberly . . . "* (Romans 12:3).

Understanding that our whole identity comes from God's grace helps us keep a right perspective on our lives and any successes we attain.

Chapter 8

Grace to Work!

"I laboured more abundantly than they all, yet not I,
but the grace of God which was with me."
(1 Corinthians 15:10)

To Do Nothing?

Some interpret grace as an invitation to chill out and do
nothing for God. "If it's all by grace then why do I need to
do anything for Him?" A natural reaction perhaps to those
who imply a salvation by works, however this was not
Paul's understanding. To him it was grace that *enabled* him
to work so hard. The first part of this verse sounds very
arrogant, Paul is saying "I put more hours in than all the
other apostles." I wonder what their reaction might have
been when they heard of Paul's claims! However, Paul
knows it's not the "natural" him, but rather, "the grace of
God which was with me." For Paul, God's grace wasn't just
his salvation, his gifts, his identity – it was the strength that
enabled him to work so hard for the kingdom. He saw he
had been given a grace from God that kept him working

when others were tired. Grace sustained him to produce an incredible workload for the kingdom. Jesus too knew what it was to pray all night and then minister all day. To achieve such things there has to be a special grace from God to accomplish His purpose.

Frequently missionaries testify about how God graced and sustained them in the most testing and overwhelming situations. One time while in Africa I was talking with a someone who'd worked with a major international ministry for nearly ten years before, with their full support and blessing, launching out on his own. Knowing something of the demands that the ministry would make on its staff I asked him how he coped. His response struck me as an excellent insight, "Whilst that was where God wanted me, I had a grace on me. When the grace began to lift, I knew God was moving me on to something else." God's grace is always there for us to do His will.

Nothing You Can Do

All our work for God should be in the context of His grace. We can be assured that the Lord is going to amply reward each one of us for our service in His kingdom and that faithful service does enhance our spiritual life (1 Timothy 3:13). But we also need to be clear that we are not simply seeking to earn His approval or trying to add in any way to the free gift of our position in Christ. We can't add to what is completed in Christ. In the words of Philip Yancey, "There's nothing you can do to make Him love you more and nothing you can do to make Him love you less."

His Own Purpose and Grace

Paul in his letter to Timothy links God's purpose and grace. He *"who has saved us and called **us** with a holy calling, not according to our works, but according to His own purpose and grace which was given to us in Christ Jesus before time began ... "* (2 Timothy 1:9). In other words, Paul states, our calling is not our choosing but rather it is given to fulfil God's own purpose through the special grace He has given us. Our calling begins with God and His preordained purpose, not our own self-made ideas (Ephesians 2:10). It is in coming to God Himself that we discover the purpose to which God has graced us. Our calling is a beautiful discovery of His grace.

Paul's Word to Timothy

"You therefore, my son, be strong in the grace that is in Christ Jesus."   (2 Timothy 2:1)

Timothy clearly had a difficult task on his hands. Paul had sent him to clear up some tricky, unresolved issues. This still very young man had been asked to ordain the church "elders" and even decide which widows would and wouldn't qualify for the benefit fund. I'm not sure which issue he would have found the hardest! Naturally Timothy seemed to battle with fear and interestingly there is no mention of his father, who may well have passed away. He certainly struggled at times and Paul had to encourage him to stir up the gift that he'd received. Paul constantly prayed for him remembering the many tears his difficult ministry had cost him. He strongly urged Timothy to be strong in the grace of God – an unusual statement which is not a term used much today. We might urge strength in faith, or the Holy Spirit, or in the Word of God, but Paul here focuses on *grace*. The word "strong" here is described as meaning: to empower, enable, to be strong. We thrive and work best in an atmosphere of encouragement. Just a few words of affirmation from a significant leader can cause a whole gust of enthusiasm to inspire us to keep on going for God. The sense of approval and strength that just a few words from a trusted friend can give, will lift us way beyond their intention. Just the thought that we have someone else behind us who believes in us, recognises our calling and is truly batting for us, is so empowering. Timothy had that in Paul, but Paul also wanted him to know that from God too. Timothy could draw on an "inward" strength as God's gracious support and favour was with him.

Interestingly, on two occasions when the church in Antioch sent out apostolic ministry from their midst they were *". . . commended to the grace of God"* (Acts 14:26; 15:40). The Greek word for "commended" here, *paradidomi*, includes: to surrender, i.e. yield up, entrust, transmit, to cast, give (over, up), recommend. There's a sense here that as these enormously risky missions went out that the church trusted that the favour of God's grace would be with them. Clearly on both occasions Paul and his colleagues would have known the real strength and support of having the church behind them, but more importantly the deep sense of God's grace upon them.

Grace to Stand

"Through whom also we have access by faith into this grace in which we stand ... " (Romans 5:2)

"I have written to you briefly, exhorting and testifying that this is the true grace of God in which you stand." (1 Peter 5:12)

Paul and Peter both spoke of how our standing before God is by His grace, not by our own achievements or successes. The Strong's definition of the Greek word "stand" includes the following, "abide, appoint, continue, covenant, establish, hold up, set (up), stanch, stand (by, forth, still, up)." The same Greek word is used in Ephesians 6 to describe a believer fully armed in the battle array of spiritual warfare, firmly and resolutely standing against the enemy's devices. There's a sense of military determination not to give ground. As believers we can confidently *stand* in God's grace refusing the constant bombardment and condemnation that the enemy throws at us. It's not something we can merely hope for passively, but involves a deep determination of the heart. Sadly, many believers today struggle in exactly the opposite way. They feel a constant sense of disapproval, that they're not up to standard, that God is constantly displeased with them.

This came to me so clearly as I fellowshipped once with a well-known and extremely successful minister who I admired greatly. In a moment of real honesty he told me he felt like a bag of sinful flesh and battled constantly with a feeling of guilt. Amazed at my friends' transparency, and at the time feeling much the same way myself, I realized that even those we consider really "successful" face exactly the same struggles common to us all. We all battle with the feeling that we're not up to it. The accuser of the brethren so often prevails in the battle for our minds, but thank God that's where grace comes in! We are not strong because we've got it all together or are fulfilling whatever regulations we've set ourselves. Our strength exists because God's unmerited, undeserved favour is upon us. We're strong because we stand before Almighty God complete in the finished work of the cross. We are strong because in Christ we are accepted and approved by God. We trust that the issue of our standing is completely settled and that unless the Holy Spirit shows us otherwise, there are no outstanding issues. Everything in Him wants nothing but the very best for us! *"If God is for us, who can be against us"* (Romans 8:31). Paul made this his one and only boast, *"God forbid that I should boast except in the cross of our Lord Jesus Christ ... "* (Galatians 6:14). We have a confidence not just because a few friends are backing us up but because God Himself does! Inevitably there will be times of discipline and pruning in our lives, but we know in it all He is working all things around us to do us good and that we can be fully confident in His complete and total love for each one of us. I don't have all that much confidence in myself, but I'm learning to have total confidence in Him.

You're My Problem!

One time I was worrying about how I'd ever fulfil the call God gave me when the Holy Spirit spoke to me, "Phil, you are not *your* problem, you're *my* problem and I'm very good at sorting people like you out!" We can completely trust Him. I personally don't think any of us will get our act completely together this side of eternity; we will always only know in part. That's why we believers urgently need to recapture how God sees us in Christ. Time and time again as I get up to minister, the enemy will remind me of all my failures, of things that don't seem quite right in the meeting, that I haven't fasted enough or if I have, that everyone else hasn't! At times like that I have to draw deeply on the inner knowledge in my spirit that my strength is in His grace not in my performance. Often it's the case that the greater the accusation, the greater the subsequent blessing on the meeting! I've almost come to see it as an incentive to really go for it!

At times I look back over my life and wonder how God ever blessed me so much! When I first spoke in tongues around six months after my conversion, the answer to everything was to pray in tongues! My counsel to whoever was crazy enough to come to me was to get them to pray in tongues! But you know, in my zeal and immaturity God blessed me. I look back and think how gracious He was to me! No doubt one day I'll look back and think how gracious He is to me now! So many struggle to accept that the Father's grace is upon them right now. Yes, of course God wants to change us and conform us further into His image, but have we stopped to realise that right now, with all our quirks and idiosyncrasies, God loves us, accepts us and wants to use us. Our confidence is that He looks at us graciously. There's a real need for us to go back again and again to the cross and be strong in His totally undeserved grace towards us.

The Father's Delight

Have you ever seen a happy family with their newborn baby? The baby can do nothing productive for the family, but their delight is just in having a beautiful child. Sure the baby's going to change and grow and no doubt there will be tensions and struggles along the way, but that in no way dampens the parents' joy. Many feel the Father will delight in them "one day", which never seems to come – maybe when we have reached the point of full maturity and total sanctification! Yet, just as a little baby will, to the delight of his or her parents, learn to walk, and that not without many falls and cuts and bruises, likewise God takes us step by step, dealing with one issue at a time, knowing if He showed us all our failings at once we would be utterly overwhelmed. At each step forward He delights in our development. Like a parent His delight isn't withheld until we reach full maturity, for in Christ He fully accepts us right now in His grace even as we grow and develop under His loving and affirming hand. We need to learn at times just to enjoy God's grace and not worry about what's next. We are after all, "His workmanship," – we're in His hands to mould and make into what we are supposed to be. Perhaps sometimes we're trying to change ourselves faster than He is! In our graceless world, should it not be that among those who have found forgiveness and life, we demonstrate how joyfully accepting God's grace is? In all our desire to change, let's stop, reflect and enjoy Christ's incredible grace to us, even right now on our journey of transformation.

The Throne of Grace

"Let us therefore come boldly to the throne of grace, that we may obtain mercy and find grace to help in time of need." (Hebrews 4:16)

In Bible times entering the presence of a king was an extremely scary thing. If you got it wrong you might not come out alive! One treated a ruler with the uttermost courtesy and respect. Interestingly in the book of the New Testament that links our new position in Christ to the practices and procedures of the Old Covenant, we are urged to "come boldly" to Christ's throne. No worming about in the outer courts, but an exhortation to come boldly in. Sometimes we think that by grovelling about before the Father we're being humble, whereas in fact we're really undermining Christ's marvellous work of redemption. I believe true humility is simply accepting with childlike faith what He has given us in Christ and living in the good of it! Christ is not impressed by our worming about in unbelief. I sense He must get frustrated at times and wants to say, "For goodness sake get up, believe what I have done for you and come on in!" Often thrones were places of judgement, therefore not places you would naturally want to go to. God's throne however, is a "throne of grace". It's a place of His favour, a place where we can come for help and comfort in time of need. The Father wants us to know His throne room is completely different.

Family Privileges

I once heard a story of a president who held a key meeting with his top national leaders; he gave strict instructions to his staff that they were not to be disturbed. Half-way through the meeting however a little eight-year-old boy walked in, straight past all the staff and the other leaders. He then proceeded to wander up to the president and jumped on his lap, where, in the middle of the business session, he received a welcoming hug! Not many people get to ever shake the hand of a president, but this boy got a hug on his lap. The reason of course was because he was the president's son and could come in any time, just because he was "family". Under the grace of the New Testament we are no longer just servants or a friend of God, we've been placed in the highest position imaginable, adopted as His sons; we're now "family". A whole new level of intimacy occurs when you are family, there's special a bond. Yes, we remain in awe and godly fear because we're bonded to Almighty God. However, Almighty God has chosen to make us His children, with all the intimate delights and privileges that brings. I sense He would say, "Please don't grovel about outside, please don't behave like an outsider with Me, come into My presence boldly because that's where you belong and that's where you can encounter my grace." There is however only one way into His Holy presence. Not our achievements, own righteousness or good works, but by faith in blood of Christ. As Hebrews states, *"Therefore, brethren, having boldness to enter the Holiest by the blood of Jesus, by a new and living way . . . "* (Hebrews 10:19–20).

In the Old Testament, priests would show the blood of bulls and goats as they entered God's presence. Today as we seek to enter His Holy Place the only acceptable passport is faith in Jesus' shed blood which puts us in perfect standing with God. There's no room for human aggrandisement in the Holy Place! Interestingly, this is the second time in Hebrews we are exhorted to come before Him with boldness. It seems as though the Father can't stress it enough, "You are mine, come to Me with boldness!" One of the first things to happen after the crucifixion of Christ was that the curtain in the temple was torn in two. Somehow I sense a bit of divine frustration in having to dwell in a building behind a curtain. I think He longed to get away from all that and come to dwell in us by His Spirit – a "new and living way". Grace teaches us the Father longs to be approached by His sons.

Chapter 9

The Purpose of the Law

Our Legal Standing Before God

Sometimes standing in grace can seem hard to grasp in contrast to the law. Just how can we have such confidence before God? It's important that we see clearly how we can now live in the good of the complete fulfilment of all of the requirements of God's Law. Romans teaches us, *"The law is holy, and the commandment holy and just and good"* (Romans 7:12). The Law was perfect and in the words of Jesus, *"One jot or one tittle will by no means pass from the law till all is fulfilled"* (Matthew 5:18). Given as it was to Israel, it represented the totality of God's requirements for mankind to stand innocent before Him. However, the standards of the law were so extremely high that no one, except Christ, could ever live up to all of them. James states how the Law demands total fulfilment if someone is to attempt to stand before God through it, *"For whoever shall keep the whole law, and yet stumble in **one point**, he is guilty of all"* (James 2:10). There is no mercy here, just one shortcoming and you're guilty of breaking the whole Law. The Law is seen as a single, complete entity; it cannot be broken up into bits so we observe only the parts we feel are relevant to us. If you're going to attempt to stand before God through your obedience to the Law, there is no second chance. It's like walking on a tight rope over Niagara Falls, one mistake and it's all over!

In the view of the above it's sometimes difficult for us to understand the purpose of the law in the light of the New Covenant. Paul gives us three purposes in Galatians 3:19–25:

1. **It reveals to us what is right.**
   Paul said regarding the purpose of the Law that, *"It was added because of transgressions, till the Seed should come ... we were kept under guard by the law"* (Galatians 3:19–23). Because of our transgressions the Law acted as a restrainer of sin. To those who knew the Law it kept them "under guard" from the potential problems of lawlessness.

2. **It shows that everyone is guilty before God.**
   "But the Scripture has confined all under sin, that the promise by faith in Jesus Christ might be given to those who believe" (Galatians 3:22). Romans states this even more strongly, *"Now we know that whatever the law says, it says to those who are under the law, that every mouth may be silenced and the whole world held accountable to God"* (Romans 3:19 NIV). The Law completely destroys the argument that says, "I'm good enough for God." Once and for all God has given His requirements; if we think we can stand through our own goodness, we have to score 100% against the

requirements God has laid down. Effectively the Law declares that, "all the world" is guilty before God.

3. **It points us towards Christ.**

   "Therefore the Law has become our tutor to lead us to Christ, so that we may be justified by faith. But now that faith has come, we are no longer under a tutor" (Galatians 3:24–25 NASB). The word for "tutor" speaks of a household servant who escorts a guest from the doorway of a large house to the host. The role of the servant is then ended. The Law shows us the complete fallacy of the notion that our own righteousness brings us to Christ. Christ is the only one who completely fulfilled the Law. It shows us our total dependence on His provision at the Cross.

Christ Is the End of the Law

In Romans Paul speaks of how we should relate to the Law in the New Covenant. He asserts, *"Christ is the end of the law so that there may be righteousness for everyone who believes"* (Romans 10:4 NIV). The celebrated professor F.F. Bruce, states that "end" can mean "goal" or "terminus". He goes on to state, " ... as Paul says, the Law was a temporary provision; the coming of Christ meant that the period of its validity was now at an end." We need to be clear here, we are no longer "under" the Law in any shape or form. As Colossians 2:13 explains, Christ wiped away all the requirements or ordinances of the Law at the cross. As Derek Prince explains, "that this 'wiping out' includes the Ten Commandments is confirmed by Paul later in the same chapter." *"Therefore do not let anyone judge you by what you eat or drink, or with regard to a religious festival, a New Moon celebration or a Sabbath day"* (Colossians 2:16 NIV). The keeping of the Sabbath is also included, being one of the Ten Commandments. The word therefore at the opening of this verse indicates a direct connection with what had been stated two verses earlier – that is, the wiping out of the ordinances of the Law through the death of Christ.

New Husband

Paul uncompromisingly states, *"Therefore, my brethren, you also have become dead to the law through the body of Christ, that you may be married to another – to Him who was raised from the dead, that we should bear fruit to God"* (Romans 7:4 NASB). We have died to the Law and are no longer under it; instead we are joined in marriage to Christ, we are in relationship with Him. Paul here compares being under the Law to someone's relationship to their husband. When the husband dies they are free to marry another. Our old husband, the Law, has died and we are now married to Christ. How shameful if we should want to go back to our old husband!

Beginning at the End!

Imagine a marathon runner coming to the end of a 25 mile race. Exhausted he just musters enough energy to cross the finishing line to win the race. However on receiving his

reward, he then hands it to *you* and lets *you* claim all the
benefits that would otherwise go to him. The good news is
this, in Christ you begin at the end of the race! Christ has run
and won the near impossible marathon of fulfilling the Law.
You now begin at the end, as if you had fulfilled the Law
perfectly. Imagine you really had perfectly fulfilled the Law,
I'm sure you'd feel pretty good. You would have a
tremendous sense of confidence. The wonderful truth is you
can have confidence before God, because in Christ it is as if
you had perfectly fulfilled the Law. You are justified, just as
if you had never sinned and fallen short of the Law. In
Romans 3:21–22 Paul explains that, *"But now apart from
the Law the righteousness of God has been manifested, being
witnessed by the Law and the Prophets, even the
righteousness of God through faith in Jesus Christ for all
those who believe"* (Romans 3:21–22 NASB). God didn't just
give us any old righteousness, He gave us, "even the
righteousness of God" – in other words, the very
righteousness of God Himself. We have every reason to have
confidence now! Amazingly, you begin your Christian life in
His completed victory! You begin at the finishing line! It's
ours for us to live in the good of it. We start where He left
off, as if we had personally fulfilled all the requirements of
the Law! It must be an enormous frustration to God when we
go back and try to do what He has already done!

A New Basis for Life

The Law is completely powerless to free us from sin.
However, *"For what the Law could not do, weak as it was*

through the flesh, God did: sending His own Son in the likeness of sinful flesh and as an offering for sin, He condemned sin in the flesh, so that the requirement of the Law might be fulfilled in us, who do not walk according to the flesh but according to the Spirit" (Romans 8:3–4 NASB). We are no longer under the law but are now freed to live in His resurrection power. *"For the law of the Spirit of life in Christ Jesus has set you free from the law of sin and of death"* (Romans 8:2). We now have a whole new way of approaching our life with God. Derek Prince likens it to the difference between having a map and a personal guide. Under the Law one is given a complete and perfect map that if followed in every detail, faultlessly, will direct the person to heaven. But no human has ever faultlessly made the journey! Under grace we're given a personal guide who has already perfectly completed the journey and has a perfect knowledge of the way. Galatians 5:18 declares, *"If you are led by the Spirit, you are not under law."*

Some, perhaps frightened of the charge of "antinomianism" (lawlessness) have tried to divide up the law into different segments. Thomas Aquinas divided the law into three: *moral, ceremonial* and *judicial laws.* This was carried out in part even by the Reformers, who frequently taught, "that while a man in Christ is not under law [meaning moral law] as a means of salvation, he remains under it as a rule of life." F.F. Bruce comments, "In its own right, this distinction may be cogently maintained as a principle of Christian theology and ethics, but it should not be imagined that it has Pauline authority. According to Paul, the believer is not under the law as a rule of life – unless one thinks of the law of love, and that is a completely different kind of law ... " Bruce is referring of course to Paul understanding how the law is fulfilled now, *"Owe no one anything except to love one another, for he who loves his neighbour has fulfilled the law"* (Romans 13:8 NASB). Something in us can struggle with all this. Some might complain, "Just give me the rules to this Christian life, that's much simpler." Mercifully Christ wants you to have more than mere rules, He's given you Himself! God is no longer the distant Law-giver, He is Emmanuel, God with us, or more exactly God in us.

That I Might Live to God

> *"For I through the law died to the law that I might live to God."* (Galatians 2:19)

The purpose of no longer being under the Law is, "to live for God". We are freed from the Law, from worrying about whether we're up to various requirements, and given a clean base from which to start, so we can now completely focus on living for God. The negative is dealt with; the law fulfilled and brought to an end. All God's requirements have been met, now we can focus on our calling and on fulfilling our destiny in God. We're no longer worrying about food, Sabbaths, and whatever other requirements we have imposed on ourselves. *All God's requirements are met. Now we can get on with positively serving God!*

Chapter 10

Freed to Serve

A Natural Response to Grace

The New Testament teaches that the "work" that we carry out in service to the Father is now based on a totally different foundation. We no longer grudgingly serving God, trying to fulfil various demands, but freely responding to the One who has met every requirement for us.

Once there was a slave standing for sale in the marketplace. Bidding was not going well, but eventually a man put in a sealing bid. As he took the slave away, she shouted insults at him and spat on him. This drew little response. Then out of sight of the market and much to the slave's surprise, the man undid the chains. The slave at first didn't understand, but then gradually the truth began to sink in, she had been set free. Overwhelmed by the man's generosity, knowing him to be man of integrity, she fell at his feet and exclaimed, "I will serve you forever." The context of her service was now completely different. Instead of the grudging service of forced slavery, it was a work of gratitude and thankfulness, genuinely wanting to help the one who'd helped her.

As we begin to realise the full extent of what the Lord has done for us in setting us completely free, our work for Him is no longer a chore or a bondage, but an act of worshipful thanksgiving. Slavery to God's work is not an act of compulsion, but rather we voluntarily like Paul give ourselves as "a bondservant of God" (Titus 1:1). The great and highly sacrificial missionary pioneer C.T. Studd summed it up in his own unique way, "If Jesus Christ be God and He died for me, no sacrifice can be too great for me to make for Him." True service in the kingdom is a response to His grace, not a means of earning it.

Living in the Positive

Being under the Law means we are still trying to live up to its various requirements. Being under grace means that all the requirements of the Law have now been met, so I can give myself positively to serve God. This completely alters how I live. The two approaches are total opposites in our attitude to serving God:

- Law asks, "What must I do to be OK?"
- Grace says, "God has made me OK, now how can I serve Him?"

- Law asks, "How much time must I spend with the Lord each day?"
- Grace says, "I love God so much I just want to spend time with Him"

- Law asks, "How much time and money must I give?"
- Grace says, "Thank You Father for all You've given me, now I want to give myself in service to You"

- Law says, "Don't commit adultery"
- Grace says, "I don't even want to look at a woman lustfully"

- Law says, "Don't steal"
- Grace says, "How can I give to those in need?"

- Law asks, "How many times must I forgive?"
- Grace says, "I've been so forgiven I just liberally pass it on"

- Law asks, "Do I have to forgive my enemies?"
- Grace says, "Love, pray and do good to your enemies"

- Law says, "Must I?"
- Grace says, "Can I?"

Law is predominantly about the negative – the don'ts. Grace is totally positive – the do's.

A Willing Obedience

As New Testament believers blessed with such an abundant gift of grace, our work for God should never be carried out under compulsion or grudgingly, but rather as an overflow of thanksgiving to God. I'm sure the freed slave who willingly gave herself in service to her redeemer actually worked far harder than she would have done as a forced slave. Knowing the kindness of Christ's grace should cause us to give ourselves to greater wholehearted service to our redeemer with a similar motive.

New Testament Fulfilment of the Law

> *"Owe nothing to anyone except to love one another; for he who loves his neighbour has fulfilled the law."*
>
> (Romans 13:8)

Paul describes how under the New Covenant the real purpose of the Law can be fulfilled in one word: *love*. Now the outward requirements of the Law are met we can concentrate on the real heart of it, to love. Jesus summarised the entire Law by distilling it down to the two most important commandments:

> *"Then one of them, a lawyer, asked Him a question, testing Him, and saying, 'Teacher, which is the great commandment in the Law?' Jesus replied, 'Love the LORD your God with all your heart and with all your soul and with all your mind.' This is the first and greatest commandment. And the second is like it: 'Love your neighbor as yourself.' All the Law and the Prophets hang on these two commandments."* (Matthew 22:35–40)

Works Are Not the Foundation

Our work for God then should be an expression of the grace that has been given to us. Work can never be seen as a way of earning grace or our salvation. Paul makes it abundantly clear that we cannot mix the two as a foundation for our salvation, *"And if by grace, then it is no longer by works; if it were, grace would no longer be grace. But if by works, then it is no longer grace; if it were work would no longer be work"* (Romans 11:6 NIV). Works as Christ so powerfully declares in the last few verses of the Bible (Revelation 22:12) will be amply rewarded, but can never be seen as a means of salvation. We need to know that we know, not just in our minds but deeply in our hearts that our salvation and ongoing standing with God is in His grace and not our works. The gospel plus anything, is always the gospel minused! When we add our own requirements to it, we in fact take away the real power of it!

Christ Is Not a Desperado

Listen to some appeals for Christian service and you would think Jesus was totally desperate. Whilst God does call us to service, to seek Him and discover our destiny, He's not some desperado begging us to serve in whatever way we choose. Yes, He's looking for obedience, but just as importantly He looks for *willing* obedience. Under grace we should no longer work grudgingly, or as many do, miserably. Our response needs to be a joyful throwing of ourselves into God's work, responding to the overwhelming goodness of the grace we've been so freely granted. Obedience is only part of the key to the blessing of God, under grace He looks for willing hearts, a cheerful giving of ourselves. Scripture tells us that both of these are vital if we are to truly see His blessing upon us.

> *"If you are willing and obedient,*
>   *you will eat the best from the land ..."*

(Isaiah 1:19 NIV)

Chapter 11

Falling from Grace

"I am astonished that you are so quickly deserting the one who called you by the grace of Christ and are turning to a different gospel."   (Galatians 1:6 NIV)

"You who are trying to be justified by law have been alienated from Christ; you have fallen away from grace."   (Galatians 5:4 NIV)

In writing to the Galatians Paul is at his toughest, in one place even suggesting certain legalists in the church should emasculate themselves completely! He appears more deeply distressed by what has crept in among the Galatians than the disastrous moral lapses of the Corinthians. Outwardly the Galatians probably appeared good, moral, upright Christians, but inwardly there had been a deep inner change that now threatened the very foundation of their faith. Paul states that the church is in danger of falling from grace. A serious charge indeed, but what did Paul mean? Few commentators argue he meant they had lost their salvation, but rather that they no longer were standing in God's grace. They had fallen from that place where they stood before God in Christ, solely and completely in His wonderful grace. They were striving to stand before Him on the grounds of their conformity to various laws. They were now, *"... seeking to establish their own righteousness, having not submitted to the righteousness of God"* (Romans 10:3).

Outward and Inward Falls

Corinthian-type moral problems are fairly self-evident and easier to spot within a church. They are outward, visible sins, and to those committed to basic Bible standards, fairly easy to address. However, the Galatian problem is inward and requires much greater spiritual discernment. This is the area Paul seems to consider the more serious, yet it is barely mentioned in today's church. How many times have you heard a pastor of a church disciplining a member because they were becoming too legalistic or self-righteous?! The focus is largely on the outward, obvious sins which are naturally important. In contrast however, Jesus seemed to largely focus on the inner issues of the heart, seeing them as the root of all outward problems (Matthew 15:19 NIV).

Clearly we don't have many Jewish believers exhorting us to submit to the Mosaic Law and telling us we're not saved if we don't. Nevertheless, is there still a Galatian problem lurking in our churches? How do we see our position before

God? On what basis do we think we gain God's approval? Are we standing before God solely by His grace? Have we slipped from Paul's simple position of grace outlined in Romans? Has a work-based standing taken the place of grace in our hearts?

The Danger that Lurks Within

I believe the Galatian problem is alive and well and many of us are susceptible to it. At one point in my Christian life I really believed I had arrived. My life seemed so together with regular fasting and a good devotional life. I laboured hard in the ministry and there were no "major" outward sins besetting my life. Yet I appeared to be unusually estranged from Christ. Something was missing. I sensed His presence wasn't as real as before. Gradually over time I realised something subtle had slipped into my life. I had slipped from my grace standing. I began to think Christ *must* accept me, that I deserved to be blessed, that my good work had *earned* me approval before God and somehow I was just one peck above many of my fellow, less spiritual, believers. Perhaps too a little bit of the elder brother spirit was affecting my heart. I was no longer just depending on grace and somehow was no longer looking just to Christ's finished work on the cross. I had added my bit to it too! My "impressive" performance actually had become a barrier in my relationship with the Father. Grace was no longer the only basis on which I felt I was accepted. In a sense I had "fallen" from my position of grace. Over time and through a number of different humbling circumstances I eventually began to know again my position of grace before the Father. God's grace, demands only our faith in Him. It is a simple childlike trust that keeps me aware again and again, that it's by grace I stand.

In today's church perhaps there is more of a Galatian problem than we might actually realise. So often the preaching that comes from our pulpits appears to paint a picture that if we are good enough God *has* to bless us. The principles of Scripture are clear, that whatever we sow, we shall reap, and that God does respond to our faith. These are principles by which the Kingdom operates. But it is easy to find ourselves in a place where our faith seems devoid of God's grace. Over time, the overwhelming sense of gratitude before God that we once felt begins to wane and die. We lose the sense of where we have come from and appear more like the "self-righteous" Simon than the worshipful woman pouring her life's savings over the feet of Jesus. But if we develop self-righteous forms of behaviour our lives can begin to fulfil the words of Jesus, "whom little is forgiven, the same loves little." In doing so we are leaving Jesus with no water for His feet, no kiss of greeting, no anointing with oil. Keeping grace fresh in our minds, helps us keep a right sense of worship before Him. We can slip from that loving thankfulness to God to a place where we can almost think He is lucky to have someone as upright as us to represent Him on earth! We are in danger of falling from grace and finding ourselves, "estranged from Christ". I am convinced this is a far deeper problem in the body of Christ than we realise. It is an enormous barrier to Christ being able to truly lavish us with His blessing and goodness as He would like to. Somehow in it all we can lose the true sense of "Good News" in the gospel and relegate ourselves to a life of approval gained by our deeds.

New Laws?

Whilst clearly a disciplined life is extremely important as we "work out our salvation" and time spent "in the secret place" with the Lord is vital for our ongoing relationship with Christ, we can easily replace our relationship with Him with attempts to fulfil a variety of self-imposed "laws". Inevitably though, there are days when we don't achieve the standards we aspire to, resulting in a nose-dive into a sense of failure and a perception of God's "disapproval". We feel good when we are hitting our targets – "I feel OK today because I had an hour quiet time … I'm doing great because I'm right up to date with my Bible reading programme … etc." – but not so good when we fail. Michael Eaton elaborates on this, "There are many Christians who are 'under the law'. They may not be well-informed about Mosaic Law, but many Christians try to 'live up to God's standards' and feel condemned by failure. Or they have a list of things that they feel God requires of them if they are to be spiritual." In his article, "True (and false) transformation", John Ortberg explains that our devotional life can be reduced to a law-bound measure of our spirituality, "As I was growing up, having 'quiet time' became a boundary marker, a measure of spiritual growth. If someone had asked me about my spiritual life, I would immediately think, have I been having a regular and lengthy quiet time? My initial thought was not, 'Am I growing more loving towards God and toward people?'"

Personally I do use a annual Bible reading scheme and regularly fast and pray, but the aim of a disciplined devotional life is not to feel good because we have fulfilled some set time span, but rather to grow closer to God and fall more deeply in love with Jesus and with each other. The cry of some is, "Just give me laws to live by," but the maturity of grace is a calling into a relationship. When Paul stated, *"Stand fast therefore in the liberty by which Christ has made us free, and do not be entangled again with a yoke of bondage"* (Galatians 5:1 NIV), he was not talking about some form of spiritual bondage, but rather returning to live under the legalism of the Law. He strongly urged the Galatians to establish the foundation of freedom that only the true gospel of Christ could give. The same applies to us today: "Stand fast" in your freedom and having discovered God's grace at salvation, don't allow yourself to be entangled again in "laws" that are not biblical requirements and will ultimately put you in bondage.

Written on Our Hearts

When I was a child my mother firmly laid down a law, "Do not touch the top of the cooker." I had no real understanding of this law, except on one memorable occasion when I disobeyed it! Having grown up, I am no longer under my mother's law, and as an adult I can put my hand on as many cooker tops as I like! However, while I'm not "under" that law now, I do have an internal understanding of it. I don't touch hot stoves because I understand the consequences of doing so! As Christians we are no longer under the Law, but in relationship to the Holy Spirit we begin to fulfil the real heart of the Law-giver. God's ways are no longer decrees written on stones, but rather written on our hearts by the Holy Spirit (2 Corinthians 3:3). Paul summed this up by saying, *"Walk in the Spirit, and you shall not fulfil the lust of the flesh"* (Galatians 5:16). By putting ourselves under various laws we are approaching our new life in Christ in an entirely wrong way.

New Testament Requirements

Interestingly the New Testament is remarkably silent on what is expected of the believer's devotional life. Jesus merely mentions, *"But when you pray, go into your room, close the door and pray to your Father, who is unseen. Then your Father, who sees what us done in secret, will reward you"* (Matthew 6:6 NIV). He also mentions, *"When you fast ... "* (Matthew 6:16 NIV), which clearly implies that believers should fast, but there are no dogmatic laws regarding spiritual requirements which a follower of Christ must attain to in their devotional life. Times of fasting and Bible reading programmes are helpful "tools" in our relationship with the Father, but these are only a means to an end, not the end in themselves and certainly not requirements demanded by Jesus.

In our marriage, my wife Caroline and I always seek to spend time together. We love each other and enjoy each other's company. However I've never calculated how much time we spend together and used that as a barometer to assess the strength of our relationship. It's our love for each other and partnership together that really makes our relationship work. It may be good to have guidelines, but the measure of the time we spend in prayer and devotion is not a law to decide if we're up to scratch. Our time with the Father is a natural overflow of our loving desire to be with Him. That's the heart of New Testament teaching. We could follow all the "laws" of modern evangelicalism and miss the heart – our purpose, our relationship with the Father.

God's Grace to You

When a friend of mine was asked how long his devotional times were each morning he was wise to not say. He felt God had clearly shown him and given him the grace to spend a certain length of time with the Father each morning. But his grace could be someone else's bondage. Many great Pentecostal leaders have had very different approaches to their devotional lives. Smith Wigglesworth for instance, said that he never prayed for more than half an hour at a time, but that he never went more than half an hour without praying. On the other hand, Paul Yongi Cho says, "I never start my day unless I have been praying for two hours." So who is right? Is one more spiritual than the other? I believe God simply graces each person differently. Legalism can occur when we impose *our* grace on others, or when we blindly imitate the devotional call of another. The

Bible doesn't regulate our walk with Christ, it only gives us guidelines. It's for each one of us to find how to draw close to the Father in love and walk in relationship with Him.

Abusing Grace

"For certain men have crept in unnoticed, who long ago were marked out for this condemnation, ungodly men, who turn the grace of our God into lewdness and deny the only Lord God and our Lord Jesus Christ." (Jude 1:4 NIV)

Sadly, it is possible to abuse God's grace. Having known a number of really generous people over the years, it's sad on occasions to see how people try to exploit their natural generosity. Similarly, false teachers (who still appear at times today) can abuse the wonder of God's grace by preaching it as a licence to sin. Their response to grace is to respond not with loving service but rather, "Well I can get away with anything then." The question does in a sense have legitimacy about it, as the great reformed teacher Martyn Lloyd-Jones once said, "If people don't ask the question, we probably haven't preached the gospel properly!" Paul however strongly addressed this problem with the Romans, *"What shall we say then? Shall we continue in sin that grace may abound? Certainly not! How shall we who died to sin live any longer in it? Or do you not know that as many of us as were baptized into Christ Jesus were baptized into His death?"* (Romans 6:1–3 NIV). Paul emphasises that becoming flippant about sin is absolutely *not* the way to respond to Christ's grace. Perish the thought.

Different translations express Paul's thoughts equally strongly: "by no means ... God forbid ... Of course not! ... May it never be ..." Clearly this would be a wholly erroneous response to grace. Paul makes it clear that by deliberately going on sinning in response to God's grace, we are denying the full power of our redemption and the new identity His grace has given us.

This point of doctrine would be the most obvious place, if he was going to do it, for Paul to threaten those who wanted to continue sinning with judgement or loss of salvation. Instead he chooses to focus on their redemptive position. He states that in Christ we have "died to sin". Paul wonders how anyone would want to, "live any longer in it?" The grace of God is clearly not something we should take lightly. If we see it as an excuse to continue to just go deliberately on living in our former way of life then perhaps we haven't really grasped grace at all. When we see the utter horror of Calvary and what our sin cost Jesus, can we really respond in such a frivolous way? The grace of God is free, but it cost Christ everything. Grace should inspire us to a life of service rather than become a licence to sin. In fact when Paul declares that living under the law gives us no power to live free from sin, he states exactly the opposite about living under grace, *"For sin shall not have dominion over you, for you are not under law but under grace"* (Romans 6:14). Living under grace by the Spirit of life in intimate relationship with the Father should release something altogether more wonderful, a life free from sin. Michael Eaton again summarizes this so well, "When you read about murder, Jesus will talk to you about anger. When you read about adultery, Jesus will talk to you about purity. You will be going *beyond* the law." Ultimately, living under grace lifts us to an altogether higher standard of life.

Our Service to God
Is Now no Longer Law Bound!

> *"But if you are led by the Spirit, you are not under the law."* (Galatians 5:18)

The Law is impersonal and has no power to free us from what it forbids. The Holy Spirit however is a personal friend and is well able to empower us to live above our sinful nature. The New Testament life is an overflow of the work of God's Spirit within our spirit, about which Paul boldly declares, *"Against such things there is no law"* (Galatians 5:23 NIV).

Again and again Paul declares that as we truly live under grace, we actually rise to a higher and more righteous lifestyle than when we merely attempt to fulfil external laws. He states that as we give the Holy Spirit pre-eminence in our lives, we will conqueror our fleshly lusts, something the Law could never promise. *"For if you live according to the sinful nature, you will die; but if by the Spirit you put to death the misdeeds of the body, you will live"* (Romans 8:13 NIV). By living under grace we truly go beyond the negative restraints of the Law to live positively, living lives of uncluttered service to our Father. By grace we enter a far richer life with our heavenly Father.

The Trust of Grace

How we respond to grace says a lot about us. Chuck Swindoll tells the story of the day he passed his driving test. His father threw the car keys to him and simply told him to come back in two hours. He wasn't going to sit next to him watching his every move any longer. He could do as he wished, burn up the highway at 100mph, jump a few red lights, or practise a few movie stunts. However, knowing the generosity and love of his father and their relationship together, he chose instead to respond sensibly to his father's trust. In grace, the gift of life is a sacred trust God has given. He doesn't force us to His ways, but rather looks for a free-will response. How we react to grace says a lot about how much we value it. Hebrews talks in strong terms of those who have turned their back on the Father's ongoing grace declaring they have, *"trampled the Son of God under foot ... treated as an unholy thing the blood of the covenant ... insulted the Spirit of grace"* (Hebrews 10:29 NIV) There's something very poignant about how the Holy Spirit is described here. It's a title: "The Spirit of grace". His character is altogether gracious. He always longs to draw us to Jesus. I know all too well that when I've missed it and made a mess of things, how gently the Holy Spirit comes alongside to convict and restore me back to that place of freedom from condemnation before God. He is in every way a Spirit of grace. Despite this, those described in Hebrews had wilfully chosen to reject the work of the Spirit. It's akin to slapping the face of your best friend who is trying to help you. God's grace should never be something that cheapens our carnality, but something that stimulates us to walk cleanly before Him with true love and devotion.

Responding to Grace

The apostle Paul responded to God's grace with a life poured out in service to God. He responded to God in the best possible way. There is nothing more tragic than grace offered in vain. It's always heartbreaking when preaching the gospel to see that so many, even those dynamically healed, don't respond to God's merciful offer of salvation. Sometimes, even when ministering in the strongest anointing, people seem to visibly harden towards God. When people come to Christ in meetings when I preach, I love to run down and shake the hand of each new Christian. Something in my heart explodes in unison with the joy of heaven. But my joy is tinged with sadness at the thought that others will leave the meeting heading for a lost eternity.

Grace in Vain?

Paul said, *"His grace toward me was not in vain"* (1 Corinthians 15:10). He made an active response to the grace that was revealed to Him. Paul was talking here in the context of his calling rather than salvation. God gives us grace for the call He puts on our life, however each call needs a response. Katherine Kuhlman, a lady who brought God's healing to so many and ministered in such closeness to the Holy Spirit, genuinely believed God called a number of others to this work ahead of her, but they missed the opportunity by failing to respond to God. Reinhard Bonnke, a man who ministers to millions, said that when he first received the call to minister in crusade evangelism, it was the same month that an established crusade evangelist decided to stop. The grace of God's call does not seem to wait forever. His purpose will go on, with us or without us. I couldn't make the point better than Paul when he later pleaded with the same Corinthian church, *"As God's fellow workers we urge you not to receive God's grace in vain"* (2 Corinthians 6:1 NIV).

Falling Short of God's Grace

> *"Make every effort to live in peace with all men and to be holy; without holiness no one will see the Lord. See to it that no one misses the grace of God and that no bitter root grows up to cause trouble and defile many."*
> (Hebrews 12:14–15 NIV)

To fall short is defined in Strong's, "to be deficient, come behind, be destitute, fail, lack, suffer need, (be in) want." The context is forgiveness in our relationships. This is an area where we often fall short of God's grace. Unforgiveness is perhaps the ultimate grace killer. It not only causes bitterness that can take root in us and defile us, but it blocks God's grace to us. Jesus was so frighteningly clear on this issue: *"For if you forgive men when they sin against you, your heavenly Father will also forgive you. But if you do not forgive men their sins, your Father will not forgive your sins"* (Matthew 6:14–15 NIV). Just as we have received grace we can be sure that our Father will give us plenty of opportunities to pass it on!

Imagine the prodigal son having returned and been thoroughly forgiven, dancing in delight with his father, amazed at his full acceptance back into the family. Perhaps there was a house worker that had wronged him before his departure. Worried about an unresolved dispute the worker may have timidly approached the son to ask for forgiveness. Naturally with all the joy and relief at his own release, it wouldn't be hard for the son to let the matter be forgiven and forgotten. The joy of his own salvation would have made that easy. However in time, as the son begins working in the fields again and playing his part in the family business, he could become a little less conscious of his forgiveness. Offences might become more easily marked and remembered. Gradually the amazing events of his restoration could become more and more distant. His initial willingness to do anything, might be not so consistent.

Once the initial euphoria of our salvation beings to wane, there can be a tendency to begin to allow our appreciation of God's grace and forgiveness to slip. Gradually the sins of others we once so easily forgave and overlooked, become harder to forgive. We begin to make more of a fuss about them. Little by little we begin to hold grudges against people. Slowly but surely, bitterness begins to defile our hearts and we begin to fall short of the grace of God.

For this reason it is so important that we keep short accounts with one another; that offences are dealt with swiftly before God and not allowed to fester and turn into bitterness. As the writer to the Hebrews said, *"Make every effort to live in peace with all men and to be holy; without holiness no one will see the Lord"* (Hebrews 12:14 NIV).

Grace's Excessive Response

In the New Testament grace asks for more than just forgiveness. Jesus did more than just forgive us and so likewise He calls us to go further, *"I say to you, love your enemies, bless those who curse you, do good to those who hate you, and pray for those who spitefully use you and persecute you, that you may be sons of your Father in heaven . . . "* (Matthew 5:43 – 45). Jesus calls for a threefold response to those who hurt us: love, bless and pray. We go beyond forgiveness, we bring them good. This is not some weird super-spiritual response to those who have hurt us. We're not called to go around bestowing a form of priestly, "Bless you my child" benediction, but rather to spiritually and practically seek the best for those who have offended us.

A pastor once shared with me how he counselled a lady in his church who was suffering at work. A promotion was coming in the office and she was due for it. However others were now acting against her in the hope they would get it instead. Her work was being unjustly criticised and she was beginning to feel the strain. How should she respond? Should she defend her work and fight? The pastor gave a more Christ-like response: to bless those who cursed her. She began on every occasion to comment positively on her colleagues' work. She helped them, gave them a lift home if need be and genuinely tried to do them good. By the time the promotion came up, the very people who tried to pull her down, recommended that she should get it, which she did. She proved a very practical outworking of Romans 12:21, *"Do not be overcome by evil, but overcome evil with good."* Jesus said of this kind of attitude that it demonstrated the qualities of sonship and equated it with true holiness (Matthew 5:48).

Chapter 12

Is There Still More?

The Danger of Pride

"For I say, through the grace given to me, to everyone who is among you, not to think of himself more highly than he ought to think, but to think soberly, as God has dealt to each one a measure of faith."

(Romans 12:3)

I will never forget my history lecturer's first lesson. His opening statement caught me off guard, "The problem with history is that we learn nothing from history!" The tragedy of church history, both ancient and modern, is that we seem to continuously repeat the mistakes of the past. Yesterday's grace is tomorrow's law, yesterday's revival becomes tomorrow's formula. It's so easy to think we have got God sussed and neatly contained in our box. The Father wants to abundantly bless each one of us;

He longs to lavish the goodness of His grace upon us. The danger is that when we are blessed, we fall into pride, forgetting that His blessing comes because of His grace and not because of anything we have done to deserve it.

As the children of Israel prepared to enter the promised land, the Lord gave them a sober warning:

> *"Lest – when you have eaten and are full, and have built beautiful houses and dwell in them; and when your herds and your flocks multiply, and your silver and your gold are multiplied, and all that you have is multiplied; when your heart is lifted up, and you forget the LORD your God ... then you say in your heart, 'My power and the might of my hand have gained me this wealth.' And you shall remember the LORD your God, for it is He who gives you power to get wealth that He may establish His covenant which He swore to your fathers, as it is this day."* (Deuteronomy 8:12–18)

The Israelites and countless others since then have done just that. I've heard it said that persecution can be easier for the believer to cope with than blessing! It is an awesome thing to walk in the blessing of Christ without becoming prideful or losing the right perspective. I love the sheer amazement of David when he looked at the awesome inheritance he had received in Jerusalem, *"Who am I, O Lord GOD? And what is my house, that You have brought me this far?"* (2 Samuel 7:18). No sense of self-achievement here, just wonder at what God had done with a rugged shepherd boy.

He Gives More Grace

Scripture gives us a foolproof way to continue to receive the grace of God. James asserts, "He gives more grace" – in other words God desires that you know the full favour and goodness of His grace. The apostle goes on to tell us how: *"God opposes the proud but gives grace to the humble"* (James 4:6 NIV). Clearly this principle was well known among the apostles as Peter quotes the same statement in 1 Peter 5:5. Being humble and staying humble before the Father enables Him to continuously pour more and more grace upon us. But when we are proud and self-righteous, trusting in our own power and might, we cause Him to resist us. He opposes us until we once again humbly acknowledge our utter dependence on His grace. Charles Finney once said, "If the Spirit of God is not allowed to break into the heart of man every two weeks he will become a hindrance to revival." Walking continuously in the grace of God requires a continuous openness and vulnerability to the Spirit – a deep "poverty of Spirit" (Matthew 5:3) that keeps us humble before Him. We will never fully arrive this side of eternity, but as we remain humble we find He continues to give "more grace".

God's Graced Apostles

"God, who was at work in the ministry of Peter as an apostle to the Jews, was also at work in my ministry as an apostle to the Gentiles." (Galatians 2:8 NIV)

Peter emerged as the leading apostle to the Jews and Paul to the Gentiles. One might have expected God to have chosen men of impeccable character and track record to become the central, foundational figures at such an early stage in the developing church. Oddly both of the leading apostles were drawn from a background of utter failure! Peter in a moment of brash self-confidence had bragged to Jesus, *"Even if all fall away on account of you, I never will"* (Matthew 26:33 NIV). But within a few hours he found himself looking into the face of Jesus having publicly denied Him three times (Luke 22:16). Peter, in the depths of utter despair, went out into the night weeping bitterly. Even so, it was to Peter that Christ entrusted a key role in leading His church. When Peter stood up to preach on the day of Pentecost, launching the spread of the gospel, it was no longer the self-confident Peter of before, but rather a man broken and humbled, and yet deeply sure of the astounding grace he had experienced at first hand. It seems Jesus would rather entrust His people to someone who clearly knew his own foundation in grace, than to someone who appeared unblemished, but who might try to stand in their own strength and confidence.

Paul, the apostle to the Gentiles, couldn't have come from a worse background. Although well-educated and taught in the Scriptures, he was so spiritually blinded that he violently persecuted the church to such an extent that he asked to be sent from Jerusalem to Damascus in order to destroy the Christian community there (Acts 9:1). His hatred of the church was an all-consuming obsession. Yet, despite all this, God broke in to his life. Imagine the utter depths Paul must have sunk to when he realised he had in fact been fighting the very God He thought he was serving. The blood on his hands was that of children of God! Yet within a few days Jesus had determined that he was, "a chosen vessel" who would take the gospel to Gentiles, kings and the nation of Israel (Acts 9:15). A truly awesome choice which even the original apostles found extremely hard to accept! However Paul at the end of himself, with no other dependence than on the grace of God, was a far more effective minister to the pagan Gentiles than the old, self-righteous Saul that he once was. In sheer wonder he later described the time of his conversion saying, *"the grace of our Lord was poured out on me abundantly"* (1 Timothy 1:14 NIV). It's as we come to an end of ourselves, that we really encounter the merciful abundance of God's grace. When we've really tasted His grace personally, that's when we can effectively minister it. The Father's choice of both Peter and Paul reflects how highly He wanted leaders who not only understood His grace, but who also had a very personal experience of it.

Paul's Growing Perspective

Paul received first hand from the Father the great "in Christ" revelation, seeing the awesome benefits bestowed on each believer. He knew so clearly his redemptive position. However in terms of his perspective of himself, he seemed more and more aware as he developed, of who he really was *outside* of Christ. Early in his life he described himself, *"the least of the apostles ... "* (1 Corinthians 15:9 NIV) Later he said, *"Although I am less than the least of all God's people, this grace was given me: to preach to the Gentiles the unsearchable riches of Christ"* (Ephesians 3:8 NIV). Finally towards the end of his life he made another amazing statement: *"Christ Jesus came into the world to save sinners – of whom I am the worst"* (1 Timothy 1:15 NIV). The man that taught so well the position of the believer in Christ, felt the full weight of his sin outside of Christ. When we draw close to God, arrogance declines and we begin to see ourselves more and more as a product of His grace.

The New Testament's Wonderful Obsession

It is amazing to read that one of the first and the last things Paul expresses in all of his epistles is his desire for God's grace to be upon the recipients. It is a wonderful obsession throughout the New Testament, and yet historians tell us it was largely absent from the teaching of second-century Fathers. Early believers seem to have been very familiar and well taught on the subject of grace. A real awareness of its power and necessity in each individual was clearly evident. Paul was keen to keep grace at the forefront of each believer's consciousness. Was it just a courteous way of greeting the saints? I believe it was much more than that. Paul was expressing his prayer and desire for God's grace to abound to everyone, that they would truly know afresh the overwhelming goodness of the Father. Below is a list that demonstrates the high place of grace, featured at the beginning and end of nearly every New Testament epistle. As you read the scriptures, ask the Father to impart something more of His grace to your heart.

To the Romans:

*"To all who are in Rome, beloved of God, called to be
saints: Grace to you and peace from God our Father and
the Lord Jesus Christ."* (Romans 1:7)

*"The grace of our Lord Jesus Christ be with you.
Amen."* (Romans 16:20)

*"The grace of our Lord Jesus Christ be with you all.
Amen."* (Romans 16:24)

To the Corinthians:

First epistle:

*"Grace to you and peace from God our Father and the
Lord Jesus Christ. I thank my God always concerning
you for the grace of God which was given to you by
Christ Jesus."* (1 Corinthians 1:3 – 4)

"The grace of our Lord Jesus Christ be with you."
(1 Corinthians 16:23)

Second epistle:

*"Grace to you and peace from God our Father and the
Lord Jesus Christ."* (2 Corinthians 1:2)

*"The grace of the Lord Jesus Christ, and the love of God,
and the communion of the Holy Spirit be with you all.
Amen."* (2 Corinthians 13:14)

To the Galatians:

"Grace to you and peace from God the Father and our Lord Jesus Christ." (Galatians 1:3)

"Brethren, the grace of our Lord Jesus Christ be with your spirit. Amen." (Galatians 6:18)

To the Ephesians:

"Grace to you and peace from God our Father and the Lord Jesus Christ." (Ephesians 1:2)

"Grace be with all those who love our Lord Jesus Christ in sincerity. Amen." (Ephesians 6:24)

To the Philippians:

"Grace to you and peace from God our Father and the Lord Jesus Christ." (Philippians 1:2)

"The grace of our Lord Jesus Christ be with you all. Amen." (Philippians 4:23)

To the Colossians:

"To the saints and faithful brethren in Christ who are in Colosse: Grace to you and peace from God our Father and the Lord Jesus Christ." (Colossians 1:2)

"This salutation by my own hand – Paul. Remember my chains. Grace be with you. Amen."

(Colossians 4:18)

To the Thessalonians:

First epistle:

"Grace to you and peace from God our Father and the Lord Jesus Christ." (1 Thessalonians 1:1)

"The grace of our Lord Jesus Christ be with you. Amen." (1 Thessalonians 5:28)

Second epistle:

"Grace to you and peace from God our Father and the Lord Jesus Christ." (2 Thessalonians 1:2)

"The grace of our Lord Jesus Christ be with you all. Amen." (2 Thessalonians 3:18)

To Timothy:

First epistle:

"To Timothy, a true son in the faith: 'Grace, mercy, and peace from God our Father and Jesus Christ our Lord.'"
(1 Timothy 1:2)

"Grace be with you. Amen." (1 Timothy 6:21)

Second epistle:

> *"To Timothy, a beloved son: Grace, mercy, and peace*
> *from God the Father and Christ Jesus our Lord."*
> (2 Timothy 1:2)

> *"The Lord Jesus Christ be with your spirit. Grace be*
> *with you. Amen."* (2 Timothy 4:22)

To Titus:

> *"To Titus, a true son in our common faith: Grace,*
> *mercy, and peace from God the Father and the Lord*
> *Jesus Christ our Saviour."* (Titus 1:4)

> *"All who are with me greet you. Greet those who love*
> *us in the faith. Grace be with you all. Amen."*
> (Titus 3:15)

To Philemon:

> *"Grace to you and peace from God our Father and the*
> *Lord Jesus Christ."* (Philemon 1:3)

> *"The grace of our Lord Jesus Christ be with your spirit.*
> *Amen."* (Philemon 1:25)

To the Hebrews:

> *"Grace be with you all. Amen."* (Hebrews 13:25)

Peter's epistle:
First epistle:

> *"Grace to you and peace be multiplied."*   (1 Peter 1:2)

Second epistle:

> *"Grace and peace be multiplied to you in the knowledge of God and of Jesus our Lord."*   (2 Peter 1:2)

> *"Grow in the grace and knowledge of our Lord and Saviour Jesus Christ. To Him be the glory both now and forever. Amen."*   (2 Peter 3:18)

Second epistle of John:

> *"Grace, mercy, and peace will be with you from God the Father and from the Lord Jesus Christ, the Son of the Father, in truth and love."*   (2 John 1:3)

Book of Revelation:

> *"John, to the seven churches which are in Asia: Grace to you and peace from Him who is and who was and who is to come, and from the seven Spirits who are before His throne."*   (Revelation 1:4)

Do you catch how strongly grace is emphasised? Clearly grace permeated the New Testament Church's consciousness in a way that is less apparent today. For all our techniques, technology, fresh waves and emphases, we don't appear as yet to have absorbed grace into our daily lives as the believers in the first century did.

The Final Verse of Scripture

The last word of the canon of Scripture, penned by the Apostle John near to where I'm writing this book, here on the beautiful island of Patmos, once again seeks to bestow the grace of Christ, this time to His whole body, including us!

> *"The grace of the Lord Jesus be with God's people.*
> *Amen."*   (Revelation 22:21 NIV)

Chapter 13

Grace to a Graceless World

But I'm Not Good Enough!

Talk to the average non-Christian today and you're likely to be greeted with a variety of negative responses. In my experience, by far the most frequent is, "I'm not good enough to be a Christian." It must deeply sadden Christ, the friend of sinners, that people are held from His grace by such a misconception. The foundation of our faith is not being "good". In fact quite the opposite – it's about coming to Christ in faith, admitting that we're *not* good. It begins as we see that without His mercy and grace we are utterly hopeless. Wherever we register on the "sin scale", 1% or 99%, we all fail the test. We need the totally undeserved favour of His grace. From there the sanctification process begins, but even then as one preacher put it, "Holiness is not of human origin, true holiness comes from God." As we walk with Christ, His Spirit works within us beginning the long process of bringing us into His image. The foundation remains as ever, grace.

What Is a Christian?

Much of the world is missing our message of grace. In Europe young people are leaving the established church in droves. The Christian foundation of the continent is rapidly eroding. Most have little or no idea of what a Christian really is. I remember the headmaster speaking at my primary school assemblies. As a general rule he would seek to teach us good moral values and create a positive attitude to others in our community. There's nothing wrong with that. The problem for me was that he always said, "A good Christian does this ... a good Christian does that ... " After six years of this, it was only natural for my young mind to conclude, "I'm obviously not a Christian!" In the West evangelism often involves the need to demolish a vast array of misconceptions, before the true grace of the gospel can be effectively communicated and received.

Although I am eternally grateful for the basic understanding of the Bible I received at my Sunday School, it focused mostly on the need for good outward behaviour, rather than on a relationship based on God's forgiveness and grace. It was only much later while away at a Crusader camp that I began to understand my need of a real, personal faith in Christ and the foundation of grace and forgiveness. The church generally is not known for communicating grace.

Jesus the Friend of Sinners

Some feel we must preach judgement to our increasingly godless continent. I'm sure there's a need at times for that.

Yet to a people starved of any understanding of grace, we need to really ensure we're getting the message of grace across. Jesus was known as a friend of sinners. In fact it was with the religious people, who felt they had no need of His forgiveness, that He struggled most. Wherever He went the sinners were drawn as if by an unseen magnet to Him. Scripture declares, *"For the law was given through Moses, but grace and truth came through Jesus Christ"* (John 1:17). Jesus came with "grace and truth." He came full of the undeserved blessing and forgiveness of God. The prostitutes, crooked business people and social outcasts were amazingly drawn to this Holy man. They found in Him, the first man ever who had the full right to condemn, and yet was so full of grace! How odd that one so inwardly set apart to the Father could draw such a bunch of unrighteous people! Jesus' words to the sinful woman must also have rung out to many a sinner who came to Him: "Go in peace, your sins have been forgiven." O how those weighed down with such oppression of guilt and despair found such freedom and relief in Christ. Yes He came with "truth" and He never drew back from speaking what was right at the right time – no watered down gospel here – but those close to Him could take it, because they knew in Christ they found the love and acceptance of His grace.

Grace – the Only Hope for this Generation

Looking at our world today it's frightening to see the moral and spiritual decay overwhelming society. In my various travels I've found few exceptions. Each continent seems to be flooded with darkness. I remember the elders of a village in West Africa who called me to ask if I could help get a Pentecostal church built in their village. They explained that fifteen years ago you could not find a girl who was pregnant before marriage, now there wasn't a girl in her teens who wasn't pregnant. In the Caribbean, older folk spoke of how they could, only a few decades ago, walk though the local town at night and be completely safe. Now the "Yardie" drug gangs war constantly with a nightly sound of gunfire. In Bogotá I couldn't walk more than a few yards from my hotel in case I would be the next victim of the now hourly kidnapping. In Russia control seems to have switched from the communists to the mafia. In the West the mass media has promoted a lifestyle that is light years worse than the excesses of previous generations. We are perhaps more likely than ever before to be in the "perilous times" of the last days. For the Christian it could be seen as a greatly lamentable time to live.

Once as I wondered what on earth was happening to my generation, looking back to previous eras when biblical values were more widely upheld, I felt the Holy Spirit begin to speak to me. I sensed He showed me that light becomes most effective in the greatest darkness. Placing a candle in a fully lit room has little or no effect, you hardly notice it. Put it in the middle of a room filled with darkness and it's the centre point. I sensed He showed me that this was a time when His salt and light in us could have the maximum impact. Jesus said, *"Those who are well have no need of a physician, but those who are sick. I did not come to call the righteous, but sinners, to repentance"* (Mark 2:17). Medicine is worthless to a healthy person, but when there is a breakthrough and a terminal illness can be cured, it becomes almost priceless. Our society is deeply sick, and now, perhaps more than in any other generation, desperately needs the medicine of the gospel of God's grace. Just as the power of medicine is demonstrated the most in curing the sickest person, similarly grace is shown most when ministered to the deepest sinner – to those who truly know there is no other cure. The world around us is in desperate need of God's grace. Somehow we, the church need, to realise afresh the tremendously good news grace can be to our fallen world. We believers need to allow His grace to imbibe every part of our being, so that we walk with confidence and demonstrate His goodness, and then model His Good News to our despairing world. God had a tremendous compassion towards the immoral Nineveh, declaring that they *"... cannot tell their right hand from their left ... "* (Jonah 4:11 NIV). Unlike the rather bigoted Jonah, He yearned to show this people with little or no knowledge of Him, the abundance of His mercy and grace. Today much of the moral decline that surrounds us is due to ignorance. If it is anyone's "fault" it could be seen as ours. To this generation Christ longs to pour out His mercy.

When Christ commissioned His apostles to take the gospel to the ends of the earth it was at a time of overwhelming political corruption, religious syncretism and immorality in the grip of a pagan Roman Empire. Their focus was to carry the "Good News" of God's gospel of grace, changing the hearts of men rather then merely judging them. Our focus should surely be the wonderful *answer* we possess in the Gospel, rather than simply highlighting the problem.

Perhaps it's in this sinful generation in which we live that the gospel of grace will fully demonstrate just how incomparable its power really is. Could it be to this sin-burdened and grace-famished generation, Paul's words to the Christians, living in the centre of corruption of Rome, will find there greatest fulfilment?

> *"Where sin abounded, grace abounded much more."*
>
> (Romans 5:20)

Further Information

For more information on Chiswick Christian Centre check the website:

www.chiswick.cc

To contact Phil please email him at:

phil@chiswick.cc

If you have enjoyed this book and would like to help us to send a copy of it and many other titles to needy pastors in the **Third World,** please write for further information or send your gift to:

Sovereign World Trust
PO Box 777, Tonbridge
Kent TN11 0ZS
United Kingdom

or to the **'Sovereign World'** distributor in your country.

Visit our website at **www.sovereign-world.org** for a full range of Sovereign World books.